Ben,
Happy Birthday
Week 2021!
xoxo
Dad

ETHICS 101

FROM ALTRUISM AND **UTILITARIANISM** TO **BIOETHICS** AND **POLITICAL ETHICS,** AN EXPLORATION OF THE **CONCEPTS OF RIGHT AND WRONG**

ETHICS 101

FROM **ALTRUISM** AND **UTILITARIANISM** TO **BIOETHICS** AND **POLITICAL ETHICS,** AN EXPLORATION OF THE **CONCEPTS OF RIGHT AND WRONG**

BRIAN BOONE

Adams Media

New York London Toronto Sydney New Delhi

Adams Media
An Imprint of Simon & Schuster, Inc.
57 Littlefield Street
Avon, Massachusetts 02322

First Adams Media hardcover edition NOVEMBER 2017

ADAMS MEDIA and colophon are trademarks of Simon and Schuster.

For information about special discounts for bulk purchases, please contact Simon & Schuster Special Sales at 1-866-506-1949 or business@simonandschuster.com.

The Simon & Schuster Speakers Bureau can bring authors to your live event. For more information or to book an event contact the Simon & Schuster Speakers Bureau at 1-866-248-3049 or visit our website at www.simonspeakers.com.

Interior design by Michelle Kelly

Manufactured in the United States of America

10 9 8 7 6 5 4

Library of Congress Cataloging-in-Publication Data
Boone, Brian, author.
Ethics 101 / Brian Boone.
Avon, Massachusetts: Adams Media, 2017.
Series: Adams 101.
Includes index.
LCCN 2017030570 (print) | LCCN 2017031981 (ebook) | ISBN 9781507204931 (hc) | ISBN 9781507204948 (ebook)
LCSH: Ethics. | Right and wrong. | BISAC: PHILOSOPHY / Ethics & Moral Philosophy. | PHILOSOPHY / History & Surveys / General. | REFERENCE / General.
LCC BJ1012 (ebook) | LCC BJ1012 .B58 2017 (print) | DDC 205--dc23
LC record available at https://lccn.loc.gov/2017030570

ISBN 978-1-5072-0493-1
ISBN 978-1-5072-0494-8 (ebook)

CONTENTS

INTRODUCTION

Ethics, also called moral philosophy, is the division of philosophy concerned with how a person should behave in a matter that is considered morally correct or good. It sounds like a simple idea—how to be good, and why it's important to be good—but it's a concept that has fascinated and agonized moral philosophers for more than 2,000 years.

Ethics means trying to figure out why one should behave morally, as well as understanding the motivating factors for that behavior. It also examines what, exactly, makes something "good" or "bad." For example:

- Is that sense of good or bad something that's naturally inside of us, or is that sense placed there by a divine being?
- Do we follow a moral code?
- Do we act morally because it is often in our self-interest to do so?
- Is ethical behavior all about the nature of the consequences of our actions?

Ethics are arguably the one type of philosophy that is readily applicable to daily life. Philosophy asks big questions like, "Is God real?" or "Why are we here?" But those big questions don't directly address how to live one's life. Ethics is the missing step between addressing the infiniteness of the universe and reconciling it with the daily existence of life on earth. If philosophy encourages moral behavior by asking the big "why" questions, then ethics is an exploration of that moral behavior, and it seeks to formulate concrete "what" and "how" answers to the questions that philosophy poses.

Ethics can and should be applied to regular life. You can tailor ethics to fit your life, and you can use ethics to make decisions and take actions that are morally "right" in fields such as medicine, business, and other disciplines. The use of ethics also brings up another ethical conundrum—why is it important to consider why a person should act a certain way? The answer lies in the concept of happiness. Simply stated, happiness is an outgrowth of ethics, be it one's own happiness or the happiness of others.

Whether you are a philosopher at heart or just interested in discovering why some things are "good" and some are "bad," *Ethics 101* has you covered. Let's delve into the fascinating and thought-provoking realm of ethics.

Chapter 1

ETHICS AND THE ANCIENT GREEK PHILOSOPHERS

Philosophy as we know it, at least in the Western world (Europe and the Americas) sprung up around the sixth century B.C. in Greece. The Greek schools of thought dominated philosophy and all of its subsets until the first century A.D.

In their attempts to decipher the big questions about life, universe, and humanity, the philosophers of ancient Greece incorporated all the knowledge they had at the time. They didn't see much of a distinction between the theoretical secrets of the unknown universe and the quantifiable, physical world. As such, these philosophers used every tool and discipline at their disposal, including ethics, logic, biology, the nature of art, the nature of beauty, and especially, political science. For the ancient Greeks, particularly for those in Athens, politics and public life were among the most important going concerns, and their inquiries into ethics frequently focused not just on the individual's duties but also on the proper ways to lead and govern.

Many philosophers wrote and taught in ancient Greece. But this golden era of Greek philosophy is dominated by three of the most famous and influential thinkers in Western history: Socrates, Plato, and Aristotle.

Socrates (ca. 470–399 B.C.) created much of the framework and methodology for how to approach philosophy and ethics. Among these innovations is the "Socratic method." This method is a form of discourse and discussion based entirely on two or more parties asking each other an almost endless array of questions. The goal is to find common ground and highlight any flaws in their arguments so as to get closer to some kind of truth. Socrates thought that this ability is one of the things that separated humans from the rest of the animal kingdom, for we're the only animals capable of logic and reason.

Carrying on the Socratic traditions was one of his primary students, Plato (ca. 428–348 B.C.). In Athens, Plato formed the first higher learning institution in the West, the Academy. One of his major contributions to moral philosophy is the theory of forms, which explores how humans can live a life of happiness in an ever-changing, material world.

The third pillar of ancient Greek philosophy is Aristotle (384–322 B.C.), a student of Plato's at the Academy, and later a professor at the same institution. One of his main theories deals with universals. He proposed whether there were "universals," and what they might be. This remains a major focus of ethical inquiry today.

The theories of these three philosophers created the Western philosophical canon, and represent the first major entries into the study of ethics.

PHILOSOPHY VERSUS MORAL PHILOSOPHY

A Brief History

While philosophy is ultimately the question of what is and isn't human nature, it is most definitely human nature to wonder. This is something that separates us from other creatures—we are self-aware of our existence and mortality, and we have higher brain functions that give us the ability to reason. The earliest humans most certainly wondered about the same questions that "official" philosophers and students formally posed: Why was the Earth created? What is it made of? Why are humans here? What is the purpose of it all? How can we live happy lives?

To even think about asking these questions is philosophy at its most basic and raw. Philosophers have sought to answer these questions—or at least inch closer to universal truths. These same questions have led to centuries of religious development. Most religions are like philosophy in that they are about the pursuit of answers to the "big questions"—however, religion is much more likely than philosophy to claim to *have* the answers. Philosophy is about asking questions—*always* asking questions.

Formal philosophy began in Greece in the seventh century B.C. Hundreds of years before Socrates, Plato, and Aristotle would solidify the foundations of Western thought (and even before Confucius and Buddha would do the same in the East), philosophers such as Heraclitus and Anaxagoras were considering the makeup of the universe and the nature of life. Anaxagoras, for example, wrote that "there is a portion of everything in everything." That's some very sophisticated thinking, and it's an idea that has resonated throughout the centuries of philosophy and will continue to resonate for centuries to come.

Ethics versus Morality

Morality is about the good-bad duality. In a general sense, morality refers to a code or rules in which actions are judged against how they stack up to shared values. Some things are "right," while others are "wrong." Ethics, meanwhile, refers to the rules that form those moral codes and that also come from those moral codes.

TYPES OF PHILOSOPHY

Ideas about the nature of the universe logically leads to the idea that all *people* are connected. We all occupy the same planet, and within it, individual societies and countries have their own sets of standards of behavior. Why are those standards in place? The answer is straightforward: to maintain the peace and to keep things humming along so that some, many, or all, may live lives of worth and fulfillment. This is where the philosophical branch of moral philosophy comes into play.

"Moral philosophy"—a term that is used interchangeably with ethics—is its own realm of study. It sits apart from the broad ideas of general philosophy, as well as the other branches of philosophy. In fact, there are many branches of general philosophy. The main offshoots are:

- **Metaphysics.** This is the study of all existence. This is about the really big questions. For example: Why is there life? What else is out there? Why are we here?
- **Epistemology.** This concerns the intricacies of acquiring knowledge and perception. Epistemology isn't so much about the truth so much as it is about determining how we know what we know. One question in this field might be: How do we know that what we think is the truth really is the truth?
- **Ethics.** Much more on this to come!
- **Political philosophy.** The ancient Greeks developed political philosophy in tandem with individual philosophy because, as they were laying the groundwork for democracy, it was crucial for them to determine the best way to govern so as to achieve "the greater good." Political philosophy is about the underpinnings of government and rule so as to maintain peace, prosperity, and happiness for some, many, or all.
- **Aesthetics.** This is about defining beauty, art, and other kinds of expression and appreciation thereof; the things that make being a human worthwhile.

You may have noticed that there is a hierarchy of the branches. Starting from metaphysics, the individual areas move from the biggest and broadest of questions about the biggest and broadest things, and progress down through finer and finer parts of existence. For example, metaphysics sits atop the list because it is about the study of all existence and why it is; aesthetics is at the bottom, because it's about how to improve and appreciate life itself.

THE HOWS AND WHYS OF LIFE

The philosophical branch that will be studied in this book is, of course, ethics. Ethics is about the application of philosophy. What good are answers, or at least very informed or deeply held opinions, about the nature of the universe and the meaning of life if you don't know how to apply those "truths" to how you live your day-to-day life and interact with the world around you? Ethics seeks to determine how and why one should behave in a way that is the most virtuous. At its most elemental, ethics is about doing the right thing; the philosophy behind it is about determining what those right things are, in a way that benefits the individual and society at large in a fair, just, and kind manner. In other words, ethics is about right versus wrong—both in terms of defining those extremes and how to act on the side of "right."

THE IMPORTANCE OF ETHICS

Reasons to Be Good

Ethics are obviously important constructs of civilization, born out of a primal human need to understand the world. But why, exactly, are ethics important? Because humanity needs structure to make sense out of the world. As we collect information, we order and categorize it. This helps us decode the vast and seemingly impossible-to-understand universe. Ethics is part of this ongoing crusade of decoding.

If knowledge defines the "what" of the universe, then philosophy is an attempt to unlock the "why." Ethics is then how that "why" is carried out, giving us standards, virtues, and rules by which we use to direct how we behave, both on a daily basis and in the grand scheme of things.

WHY ACT ETHICALLY?

Philosophers have pinpointed several different reasons why humans can and should act in a virtuous manner. Here are a few:

- **It's a requirement for life.** It's our biological imperative as humans to survive and thrive, and ethics are part of the complicated structure of humanity that helps us determine the best ways to act so that each of us may live a long, productive life. Acting virtuously helps ensure that our actions are not aimless, pointless, or random. By narrowing down the vastness of the universe to a lived experience with purpose and meaning—especially if it's one shared by a society or cultural group—goals and happiness are more within reach.

- **It's a requirement for society.** To be a member of society in good standing, one must follow the codes and laws that govern that culture. Everybody has a role to play, and if the social fabric breaks down, the happiness of others is threatened. Ethics builds relationships, both individually and on a grand scale. Kindness matters, and it helps forge the underlying bonds that unite a society.

- **For religious purposes.** Some people try to act in a way they have decided is the most morally upstanding, and they get their cues from religion. This plays into a type of ethics called divine command theory. People who subscribe to this type of ethics act in accordance with the rules set forth by an organized religion, and those rules are derived from holy text or the direction of a divine entity. While some religions say it is important to act appropriately just because it is the right thing to do, they also provide the crucial incentive of consequences: be good enough, and a person will reach paradise when they die; be bad enough, and an eternity of torment awaits. In other words, we need incentives to act morally.

- **For self-interest.** Some ethicists believe that humans ultimately act out of self-service, that they do things with their own interests in mind. This viewpoint even informs their moral behavior. As hinted at in "the Golden Rule" (do unto others as you would have done unto you) and the similar Eastern idea of karma, being good can be a self-serving pursuit. Hence, if a person behaves morally, respectfully, and kindly to others—for whatever reason, and even if those reasons are motivated by self-interest—good things will happen to that person in kind.

- **Because humans are good.** This is a major theme of moral philosophy. The essential question is this: Are humans ethical because they have to be, or do humans pursue a moral life because certain acts are just naturally good, or naturally bad? As an action, this plays out in the idea that humans, by and large, are themselves naturally good, and they try to act accordingly.

Virtues

Central to the discussion of ethics is the notion of virtues. Moral philosophy is very much invested in determining not only the way humans ought to act, but also the way they act. Ethics lead to quantifiable values, and those values are the handful of qualities that direct good behavior. Most every different viewpoint on ethics is concerned with virtues, because virtues have no ties to a specific religion or ethical ideology. And many are universal. (Some aren't, but that's a question for ethicists to debate.)

THE SOPHISTS

Philosophers for Hire

Sophists were professional traveling teachers who worked as free-lance tutors in Athens and other major Greek cities in the fifth century B.C. They offered—only to wealthy males—an education in virtues, which was called *arete*. They got rich but were widely resented because they had their own agenda for what to teach the children of the wealthy: warrior values such as courage and physical strength.

As Athens adopted the early vestiges of democracy later on, arete evolved to mean how to influence others, particularly citizens in political functions, through persuasion with a mastery of rhetoric, or the ability to debate and discuss. Sophistic education grew out of this and capitalized on it.

Virtues of the Sophists

Among the virtues professed by some of the Sophists were:

- **Protagoras:** Truth is relative, and so therefore everyone has their own subjective truth.
- **Gorgias:** If something does exist, we cannot ever really know it, and we have no way to communicate it.
- **Prodicus:** Wisdom is a great virtue, and those that are wise should receive more attention than the less learned.

The six main teachers in Athens at that time came to be known collectively as the Sophists. These influential philosophical thinkers wrapped up their ideas with politics, human behavior, and moral philosophy. Their names were Protagoras, Gorgias, Antiphon, Hippias, Prodicus, and Thrasymachus.

GOING WITH THE FLOW

It's difficult to fully understand the philosophy of the Sophists because, like many texts of all kinds from ancient Greece, detailed records of their works have not survived. (Most of their arguments were oral, anyhow—they were all about debate and rhetoric, not rigorous research and synthesis.) Most of what is known about them are from text fragments, Plato's withering criticism of them later on, and other secondhand writings a generation or more removed.

While all ethical arguments are subjective in their drive to find objective ends to ethical ideas, the Sophists are widely regarded as just plain wrong. This is because they often used faulty logic to explain and justify what they said were truths. In fact, their end goals were to be private tutors and to keep the wealthy and powerful wealthy and powerful. They had no interest in overarching truths about humanity. Their ethical arguments kept in line with the idea that it is moral, or rather amoral or above the concept of morality, to act as one sees fit in order to win. Happiness doesn't matter; doing the right thing doesn't matter. The only consequence that truly matters is winning.

THE DEBATE TEAM

Similarly, Sophists liked to win public speaking contests and debates, so as to increase their standing—and salary demands— among other Sophists. So they developed methods that made their arguments sound good even if they weren't truthful. But here's what we can learn from the Sophists: the importance of debate, arguing, and seeing an argument through—and by the sin of omission, being able to back those arguments up with facts or proof, or at the very least, be able to argue a point and reason through it so the argument at least makes sense.

Here's how they did it. When arguing a position in a classroom, public debate, or competition, they would offer a best "proof" in support. Ideally this would be a quotation from a great work of Greek religious literature that told of the gods and their actions. After all, if an action of the gods was found to be similar to that being discussed in debate, then that was evidence of the correctness of the action—for the gods are gods, and they are infallible. This line of argument was not completely objective, but that didn't really matter for the Sophists, because the ones who did best in these debates and discussions were those who had a mastery of quotations. Whoever could come up with his justification the fastest was seen as the smartest, and was usually the winner of the debate. A masterful Sophist like this would then get more work tutoring the son of a wealthy Athenian, and there were a whole series of practical courses that a Sophist could teach to his young charges. Among the skills the students were taught by their private philosophers were:

- How to argue and win despite a bad case
- How to charm someone to get what you want
- How to manipulate others in business deals
- How to do whatever it takes to win

IT'S A LIVING

The real kicker is that many of the Sophists didn't actually believe the stuff they espoused, namely the religious justifications and examples they used in their arguments. Sophists were most likely atheists, cynical about the Greek pantheon of gods and its traditions. But they did believe in the often crass, win-at-all-costs nature of their teachings. For them it was all about saying what Athenians wanted to hear so they could get work.

The Sophists may have shown a complete lack of ethics at the highest levels, which was damaging to humanity and democracy, but they did bring up some philosophical truths that are still being debated in ethical circles today. Socrates, Plato, and Aristotle rose up from the Sophist tradition to create legitimate, not-for-profit philosophy that set out to investigate human nature and the right ways to act. Society's demand for wisdom required more than what the Sophists offered. But at least the Sophists espoused practical application of virtues, whatever they may be, to life, which is what ethics is all about.

It's no coincidence that today the term *sophistry* has come to mean fake knowledge that sounds real because it's surrounded by the trappings of logic, knowledge, and academia. It means the deliberate use of phony reasoning.

THE SOCRATIC METHOD

How Socrates Shaped Ethics

The period in which Socrates (ca. 470–399 B.C.) lived in Athens was known as the Golden Age, in part because of Socrates's contributions to elevating human knowledge, reason, and understanding. Socrates was educated by an early philosopher named Anaxagoras, at first splitting his time between philosophy and cosmology (the study of the nature of reality, an early form of philosophy). Eventually, he switched almost entirely to philosophy. As a way to learn, he always asked questions, pestering residents of Athens to make them realize they didn't even have a moral code.

Quotable Voices

"True wisdom comes to each of us when we realize how little we understand about life, ourselves, and the world around us." —Socrates

Before Socrates streamlined philosophy and ethics to be about why humans do what they do, "philosophy" was about the intersection of metaphysics, religion, and science. But Socrates was interested in the theoretical notions that prompted all of those other fields. He was the first to assert that philosophy should be about figuring out how people should live their lives, and that the cornerstone of ethics was determining which virtues carried the most merit.

NEVER STOP ASKING QUESTIONS

It's possible that Socrates's most important legacy in the Western philosophical canon is the introduction of the dialectical method of questioning. (Socrates called it *elenchus*, which translates to "cross-examination.") It's since come to be known as the Socratic method.

The Socratic method is a savvy, scientific approach to discussing philosophical questions and highly conceptual notions. Technically, this method of inquiry is a process of negative hypothesis elimination—better points than the one raised can be found by two parties debating each other on the topic, asking questions, raising objections, and then eliminating potential possibilities as they are disproven. The Socratic method would later be adapted into the very similar scientific method that is used to determine truths about the physical world.

Socrates's Personal Life

Socrates was an academic who never stopped learning, at the detriment to his family. Married to a woman named Xanthippe and the father of three sons, he was so obsessed with his search for wisdom and knowledge that he often neglected to support his family.

The Socratic method breaks down a problem into a series of small questions. The answers help the participants craft and hone a solution, making it better and better, and more and more difficult to refute or disprove (and therefore more likely to be true). This leads to much rational thinking and the singling out of good ideas.

A VIRTUOUS LIFE

Socrates advocated a life of virtue, or arete. To Socrates, living a moral, wholesome, and decent life was in the best interest of everyone, including the individual. He felt the only way to live a life of happiness was to be morally upstanding. He reasoned that once people understood the good virtues with which to live life, then they would always do good. Because once you know what the good way is, why would you do anything else? (Socrates had a very high opinion of his fellow human beings.)

Conversely, Socrates attested that the only reason people do anything bad or unhealthy was out of moral ignorance—they aren't versed in the virtues and simply don't know any better. But if one truly makes an effort to study and understand what Socrates said were the most important virtues—courage, justice, piety, and temperance—then that person will of course make every effort to live out those virtues all the time. And this individual will be happy doing so. Socrates firmly believed that if people are educated in the moral ways, they *will* do what is right.

The Death of Socrates

Socrates so agitated the status quo that he became famous for his theories about human nature and philosophy. He was eventually condemned to death for being an atheist (not believing in the Greek pantheon) and corrupting the youths of Athens by imploring them to question everything. He had time to escape but didn't, because he thought it would be contrary to his principles (as depicted in Plato's *Crito*). He drank hemlock (a poison) and spent his last day questioning the immortality of the soul with his friends.

Within this chain of reasoning, this ultimately unrealistic scenario does make sense—after all, who would knowingly do something evil? (This conflicts mightily with Aristotle's much more realistic concept of *akrasia*, or moral weakness, which manifests in those who know what the morally correct decision is and then do something bad anyway.)

Socrates believed it was the duty of the philosopher to write, debate, and teach. In doing so, this freed others of their misconceptions, delusions, doubts, self-deceptions, and other virtue-blocking negative feelings, and got them on the road to *eudaimonia*, or happiness.

PLATO'S ETHICS

The Platonic Ideal

The scion of a prominent Athenian family, Plato (ca. 428–348 B.C.) was fortunate and bright enough to begin his academic career as a student of Socrates. After Socrates died, Plato absorbed new ideas with voyages to Egypt and Italy before returning to Athens to start his own institution called the Academy. Later a teacher to Aristotle, Plato is the second in the direct line of ancient Greek philosophers who brilliantly laid the groundwork for the complete history of Western ethical thought. Not only was he a philosopher who suggested fascinating truths about the universe and human nature—and dared to do so outside the strict confines of religion—but he nailed down what it is that makes us human: We think. We reason. He was among the first academics or thinkers to develop an analytical system that could be used to analyze information. So, in that way, he showed the West how to think about thinking!

Plato was also a moral philosopher, because at the time morality was more or less the reach of philosophy. Philosophy had not yet reached the point of the "why do we do what we do?" level of questioning—it was more about how we ought to behave in the best way possible so as to make ourselves happy and content in a world that can be confusing and cruel. The answer to this quandary? Virtues.

Of the three main Western ethical schools of thought that will be discussed in this book—deontology, consequentialism, and virtue ethics—virtue ethics is definitely the oldest. It is perhaps also the simplest to understand. Plato created a lot of the basics of virtue theory. He was of the mind that the inner moral "goodness" of something does not reside in the action itself, as it does with deontology, or in the results of those actions, as it is in consequentialism. Rather, virtue ethics focuses on who we are inside: our moral fiber, our conscious, our virtues. For Plato an action is only good in that a virtuous person takes those actions and does so from a place of deeply held conviction. In other words, the goodness is already inside you.

Virtue Ethics

Virtue ethics is the idea that ethics is about the agents, not their actions or consequences. Those agents must be in possession of positive character traits called virtues in order to act morally and have a good character.

BUILDING ON SOCRATES

Early in his career, Plato presented the teachings of Socrates in the form of dialogues, or records of conversations that Socrates had with his students or other debate partners. It's in his "middle dialogues" period that Plato really began to strike out on his own. His early dialogues are concerned mostly with asking questions. In his middle period, he provides conclusions and answers to conundrums. He kept up the dialogue format to discuss philosophical issues, expanding on ideas that Socrates first explored. For example, in the dialogue *Meno*, Plato reiterates the powerful Socratic ethical notion that no one does wrong knowingly—that they simply don't yet have the virtues that allow them to know the difference between right and wrong.

But Plato did more than reiterate that ethical notion in *Meno*, he also examined it by introducing the anamnesis, or "the doctrine of recollection." Plato asserted that humans are actually born in possession of all knowledge, and that we simply discover it along the way. It is through this that Plato explores (but doesn't really answer) the notion of whether or not virtue can be taught.

A NEW *REPUBLIC*

Plato's most influential work in his "middle dialogues" era is *The Republic*. It's a book about justice, both in an ideal government and an ideal individual. It begins with a Socratic conversation about the nature of justice before continuing into a lengthy discussion of the cardinal virtues of justice, wisdom, courage, and moderation—both in the individual and the whole of society.

He tied ethics into the political sphere, such was the importance of it to the government-centric, close-knit city state of Athens. To Plato, ethics were crucial to the concept of justice at the political level. He held that just individuals made up a just society, and that both should be driven by three main virtues: temperance, wisdom, and courage. These first three, when properly developed and balanced, result then the fourth virtue: justice.

Partially to explain what a just individual might strive for, Plato used *The Republic* to demonstrate the notion of a just city, or Kallipolis, for the sake of comparison. In this model the city is split into three classes:

- **Guardians:** These are the rulers of Kallipolis. To Plato a ruler must be someone whose chief concern is justice and truth, and who has learned more essential knowledge along the way than someone in any other class. By this, Plato means that only philosophers are truly qualified to rule.

- **Auxiliaries:** The warrior or military class, tasked with defending the city from invading enemies and with keeping the peace inside the city.
- **Producers:** The largest class of society, it's what today we'd call the working class or the middle class. Plato includes here everybody who isn't a ruler or a warrior, everyone from doctors to artists to judges to craftsmen. They are so named because they produce goods and services.

In an individual person, each of these classes corresponds to a part of his or her soul. The Guardians are wise and all-knowing, so they are reason personified. Spirit, which means the mind's emotional systems and impulses, goes along with the reactive and regulatory Auxiliary. Producers correlate to the appetitive, because both are about propagation, either of the city or the self. As justice in the city results from the ideal balance of all three classes living together (although under the rule of the Guardians), so too does Plato view individual justice, or harmony, as the different soul parts living in proper balance, but with reason ruling above all.

Quotable Voices

"There are three classes of men; lovers of wisdom, lovers of honor, and lovers of gain." —Plato

THE MORAL PHILOSOPHY OF ARISTOTLE

Creating Ethics

Aristotle (384–322 B.C.) was an Athenian philosopher in ancient Greece. A founding figure of Western philosophy, he enjoyed a special emphasis on ethics, although his system of wisdom involved all kinds of philosophical subsets, including metaphysics, aesthetics, political theory, and science. Along with his predecessors Socrates and Plato, his work forms the basis of all later Western philosophical thought, particularly medieval movements like Scholasticism and the rise of philosophy in the East—his writings were translated, spread, and interpreted in the Muslim world and in the Far East. His principles are part of a system that bears his name: Aristotelianism.

Aristotle's father was the personal physician to Macedonian king Amyntas, and so he grew up as an aristocrat and enjoyed the according benefits of education. Both of his parents died when he was a child, and at age eighteen he moved to Athens to attend Plato's Academy, a place he stayed on as a teacher for twenty years. Because Aristotle developed his own branching off of Plato's philosophies, Plato's nephew was chosen to lead the Academy, and so Aristotle left. He eventually went on to tutor the young Alexander the Great. He then returned to Athens, and outside of the city he established his own school called the Lyceum, a direct competitor to Plato's Academy.

CULTIVATING VIRTUES

The curriculum at the Lyceum was broad, but the ethical portion focused on natural philosophy. Only fragments of the works he wrote during this time survived. Among them are *Organon*, *Physics*, *Metaphysics*, *Nicomachean Ethics*, *Politics*, *De Anima*, *Rhetoric*, and *Poetics*. And only about a fifth of his entire works have survived, totaling about twelve volumes. But due to the efforts of latter scholars, editors, and compilers, we nonetheless have a pretty good representation of his contributions to ethics. While Socrates and Plato delved into ethics, they didn't give it a name or treat it as its own subject. Aristotle changed that, coming up with the word *ethics* (or rather *ethos*, the science of morals) and defining it as an attempt at a rational explanation to the universal and ongoing question of how humans ought to act and behave. Furthermore, Aristotle related political theory closely to ethics, calling politics the examination of how the government should behave and politicians should rule, and distinguishing ethics as how the *individual* should pursue good.

One of his main theories was the importance of cultivating virtues: excellent character, or arete, and its end goal, excellent conduct, or *energeia*. For Aristotle, as he wrote about in *Nicomachean Ethics*, a person with excellent character just has an inclination to do the right thing; and not only does such a person do the right thing but also does it at the right time and in the right way. Among the virtues he considered among the most admirable and desirable were bravery and temperance. Mastering these virtues means controlling one's appetites and carnal desires. More than that, Aristotle attested that acting in a good, clean, virtuous way was a method to bring absolute, undeniable pleasure. Therefore, by rejecting the pleasures of food and flesh, for example, a human would find even more happiness in temperance. This is because, for Aristotle, the highest aims are living well through virtue and the pursuit of eudaimonia, that feeling of well-being or happiness, or living one's best life, flourishing and thriving instead of merely existing. In fact, good character was the very prescription for happiness: it is a direct line.

Because Aristotle was a student of Plato, and Plato was a student of Socrates, naturally Aristotle's work was going to build on that of those influences. However, one way Aristotle veered off was in the realm of what virtues were the most important. Plato discussed four cardinal virtues: courage, temperance, justice, and prudence. But in his writings, Aristotle focused entirely on courage and temperance as the main virtues, while also discussing many second-tier virtues. Practical wisdom, or prudence, was its own thing, and something to heartily pursue. He also attested that all the highest moral virtues require each other, and all are necessary and requiring of the intellectual, or practical, value. (He also said that because of this, the happiest life and one of most virtue is that of a...philosopher.)

ACTING OVER THINKING

Ethics were not merely theoretical as far as Aristotle was concerned. You can't just have virtues and expect to be happy. Rather one has to work on getting those virtues, and work to attain those virtues, both by being trained in them and experiencing life in order to become good. In other words, actions are as important as intentions. A virtuous person should certainly study what those virtues are, but that person must also act on them and do good things. This is called practical ethics, and the logic is a bit circular: to be ethical one must learn what is ethical, and then do those things, which makes that person ethical. Conversely, he says that good actions are wasted if they are not done as part of a drive to a virtuous life. To summarize: to be ethical, one must have the intent to be ethical and then frame those actions within that ethical knowledge so as to obtain virtues. Then, he says, you'll be happy.

A SEPARATION OF THE SOUL

Like all of his Greek counterparts, Aristotle was fascinated with breaking the soul down into parts. Aristotle separated the human soul—or human nature, as we would call it now—into two parts: the rational part and irrational part. (This is similar to the idea of nature versus nurture.) The rational part includes your skills of reasoning through practical and theoretical concerns. The irrational part decides your wants, emotions, and desires. The irrational aspect of the soul is something common to all living creatures; but the rational part is something humans alone have. It is the rational part, the call to action, that is our purpose. It is our mission to reason our way to virtues, and to use virtues to get happy.

Unifying Another Discipline

In addition to philosophy, Aristotle had a profound effect on theater. His book *Poetics*, written in 335 B.C., is the oldest surviving example of dramatic theory and literary theory. It includes Aristotle's "Unities," which are three suggestions for how a stage play ideally ought to be written. The Aristotelian unities are: unity of action (a play should have one central plot, and few to no subplots), unity of time (the whole thing should take place over the course of twenty-four hours or less), and unity of place (the play should occur in one setting). Playwrights used the "Unities" as the unofficial rules of their trade for centuries.

Plato and Aristotle largely agreed that the aim of human life was happiness, and the way to get there was by living a life of reason, or by making ethical choices. But while Plato attested that virtues are naturally inside us, Aristotle thought that humans have the capacity to be virtuous, but that the virtues are earned and acquired through the practice of daily life. In other words, happiness comes by doing things ethically.

Chapter 2

THE DIVERGENT GREEK SCHOOLS

With their writings and schools, Socrates, Plato, and Aristotle established the Greek academic and philosophical tradition. They brought up so many new ideas and so many new possibilities that it led to an explosion in philosophical exploration. Many new schools, branches, and cults of personality sprung up after the Golden Age, especially as Greek culture and ideas went out into the world and came back to Greece. Somewhat like the circular logic of Aristotle's practical ethics, Greek philosophy influenced the world, and the world in turn influenced Greek philosophy. Five major philosophical and ethical schools sprung up in the Western world after the Golden Age of Athens. Instead of focusing on statecraft and governance, as the philosophical pillars of the Golden Age had done, adherents of these new branches focused instead on the life of the individual and personal ethical obligations and approaches. These five groups were:

- **The Cynics** believed that the one true purpose in life was to seek out and experience happiness.
- **The Skeptics** thought there were no moral certainties, and with it, an imperative to doubt everything.
- **The Epicureans** believed pleasure to be life's highest pursuit. But even as the sect advocated pleasure seeking,

it warned against pursuing pleasures that could also cause harm to the self and others.

- **The Stoics** believed that nature was innately rational and that humans were unable to change that powerful force. Morally, they believed that happiness could come by accepting this as truth, and so they endeavored to change their own behaviors so as to fall more in line with this idea.
- **The Neoplatonists** were in the group that was an expansion of and application of Platonic ideals but with more religious-based theological teachers and Eastern mysticism.

THE PHILOSOPHY OF THE CYNICS

Question Everything

One thing that the great philosophers of ancient Greece spent a preponderance of time on was applying the individual concepts of philosophy and ethics to political and public life. That was how important politics were to Greece—public life was all-important, and philosophy had to find a way to fit into it. Without that fitting in, philosophy would not be taken seriously, much less thrive. Philosophy was a tool that citizens and rulers alike could use to better understand themselves and other humans—and to exploit, both for personal gain or to progress society at its highest levels.

In the Hellenistic era (ca. 323–30 B.C.), chief among the changes in philosophy was a shift from political and public applications toward the explicitly personal, and how man should behave in his private, nonpolitical life. Distinct ethical schools of thought emerged. These schools helped lay the groundwork for divergent ethical theories that would develop over the next several hundred years. Perhaps the least subtle and among the more radical of these viewpoints was the philosophy set forth by the Cynics.

THIS TIME IT'S PERSONAL

The Cynics were a philosophical movement that believed the one true purpose in life was to seek out and achieve happiness. This was to be done by looking to nature for certain virtues that would increase that likelihood, and following them as nature would dictate. The term *Cynic* is of course related to the word *cynical*, which today has come to mean "a negative, distrusting disposition." This definition ties into the Cynics in that the Cynics were "cynical" of any sort of man-made system of ethics or morality. As a result, they preferred to go it the old way—the *really* old way.

Cynicism was all about denying the philosophical and ethical conventions that had been established by the mainstream thinkers—because they were false—and following what came naturally. Cynics especially wanted to condemn traditional values that had falsely become virtues, such as wealth, reputation, pleasure, property, and familial obligation. They endorsed shocking speech and action as a powerful counterpoint to those values of common decency.

COMFORT IN THE UNCOMFORTABLE

An early leader of the Cynics was Antisthenes (445–365 B.C.), born into a wealthy family that was so prominent he was able to be a student of Socrates. While Plato carried on Socrates's teaching and the dialectic method, Antisthenes liked how Plato taught "the art of enduring" and of being indifferent to external factors so as to create an independent way of living. Antisthenes taught that there are two kinds of "objects": the external, such as personal property, and the internal, which comprises truth, knowledge, and the soul. He discouraged taking pleasure in any kind of external good or pleasure that wasn't the direct result of virtue, and encouraged actively taking on discomfort, such as physical pain, to accompany and motivate the soul in its drive to become wealthy in those "inner" objects. His writings have not survived, but some of his defiant sayings have lasted through the centuries, such as "I would rather go mad than feel pleasure." Antisthenes, and his most devoted followers, took to living a life of extreme austerity to avoid any sort of temptation by the hollow pursuits of man. They lived on the street, dressed in rags, and harassed passersby about their moral choices.

Diogenes

One of Antisthenes's most important students was Diogenes (412–323 B.C.), who came to Athens from Sinope, in what is now Turkey. (He was exiled when he defaced the coinage, akin to burning the flag.) He lived out Antisthenes's theories to the extreme—he lived as a beggar, and walked the streets in a barrel, criticizing passersby on their shallow lives and adherence to arbitrary social conventions that he believed robbed them of their freedom to live according to the principles of nature.

THE SKEPTICS OF ANCIENT GREECE

Full of Doubt

To be skeptical means to openly question some kind of truth or fact, with a tendency toward disbelief of the matter in the long run. Of a similar frame of mind were the Skeptics, an ancient Greek collective of philosophers who did not believe that moral certainties could be, well, certain. They were skeptical of any and all kinds of objective morality. They saw them as either a construct of man and society or that they were simply not proven or provable to be universally or objectively true. While they respected that a good argument could be made for either side of a moral issue, they lived in a moral way and so generally tended to recommend following the prevailing social conventions as to what acts were and were not moral. It was just easier that way. In Skepticism, the name of the game was to doubt everything: not only could big truths not be proven but doubting everything was also the path to happiness.

The kind of Skepticism discussed here is often called Pyrrhonism in deference to its founder and chief architect, a Greek thinker named Pyrrho (ca. 360–270 B.C.). And that's "thinker," not "official" philosopher—Pyrrho and his school were not part of the Athenian mainstream. Not trained in Plato's Academy or any other major school, Pyrrho was a painter from the Greek coastal town of Elis. Arguably his most major philosophical influence was Eastern mysticism, which he studied when he accompanied Alexander the Great on an exploration of India.

IT'S DOUBTFUL

The main difference between Western and Eastern philosophies is that of worldview. In the West, direct, concrete answers are sought. In the East, there's more of an acceptance of both the mystery of the world and the reality that there will always be bad to go along with the good and there's nothing anyone can do to stop that. This Eastern perspective is reflected in the philosophies of Pyrrho. His view was: Don't even try to make a judgment on every matter. Or any matter. He didn't even trust his own senses, and other people had to walk him around so he didn't kill himself or trip over anything. A story about him goes that he was once on a ship that hit a storm, and everyone on board thought they were going to die. But not Pyrrho, who stayed calm and pointed to a pig on board who was oblivious. He thought this was the ideal state.

Unfortunately, since Pyrrho wasn't an academic, he didn't write anything. But his school thrived for centuries, and some works of his students survived, particularly those of a doctor named Sextus Empiricus, who wrote *Outlines of Pyrrhonism*. His definition of Skepticism, refined, is: "an ability to place appearances in opposition to judgments in any way whatever. By balancing reasons that are opposed to each other, we first reach the state of suspension of judgment, and afterwards that of tranquility." (This is the same as Pyrrho's own definition, more or less.) And that's how Skeptics approach knowledge, truth, and ethics: tentatively go with what *seems* to be the most right, if possible.

It's a simple theory, but it is vexed with the problems of any ethical argument: perception. Skeptics propose that there are always at least two ways of perceiving anything—point of view and experience. Neither is right or wrong. But if this is the case, how can an issue be decided? It's can't. One therefore can't just make the decision, suspend judgment, and move on. Skeptics sidestep this dilemma by stating that it's perfectly fine to say "I don't know." From a Skeptic's point of view that simple admission leads to happiness. Why? Because debate has been ended preemptively. If no particular perception is preeminent, then one doesn't need to be right or prove the other person wrong. Happiness ensues because there is no need to get hostile and mean. By proclaiming a fact (declaring that a given perception is true), a person opens the door for an opposing view or stressful debate, or creates turmoil in the mind as one reflects on alternatives and is wracked with even the smallest amount of doubt—with the imminent tendency to disbelieve either way regardless.

Quotable Voices

"By suspending judgment, by confining oneself to phenomena or objects as they appear, and by asserting nothing definite as to how they really are, one can escape the perplexities of life and attain an imperturbable peace of mind."
—Pyrrho

THE TEN METHODS

Pyrrhonian Skeptics devised ten different arguments or "patterns of skeptical reasoning" to show that everything can, will, and should be doubted, or rather dismissed. For any hypothetical "truth" presented, a Skeptic can knock it down. All follow this same basic pattern:

- An object seems to have (X) quality to me.
- The object seems to have (Y) quality to you.

- How is my perception any better than yours?
- It's not. Judgment is therefore suspended as to whether object is more (X) or (Y).

Therefore, these are the ten ways in which Skeptics maintain things can be perceived so differently that absolute truths cannot be determined:

- Differences in animals
- Differences in people
- Difference in sensory perception
- Difference in circumstances
- Difference in position, distance, and place
- Difference in mixtures of all of those things
- Difference in quantity and constitution of similar concepts
- Difference in relations
- Difference in relative frequency and rarity
- Differing systems, customs, laws, and religious beliefs

In the study of ethics, Skepticism is important because it is a kind of relativism—perhaps at its most pure and raw. If a Skeptic suspends judgment about the innate nature of a thing being good or bad, then he or she can make no judgments about it. It is therefore not for the Skeptic to determine virtues. Likewise, there are no objectively truthful values. You, as a Skeptic, might sense something as being unjust, but that doesn't matter. What prevents people from committing unjust acts are the ethicists who make laws based on their own perceptions. And so, to live in society we fall back onto customs, because it's the way it's always been done.

THE EPICUREANS

Go for the Good, Avoid the Bad

Today, the word *epicurean* has come to be associated with luxurious living and people who take pleasure in cooking and eating. This is because eating well is pleasurable. In classical reasoning an Epicurean was someone who equated anything pleasurable with it being good. Conversely, what's painful is objectively bad for an Epicurean. Therefore, bad things should be eschewed, things that feel good should be pursued, and happiness is obtained through the seeking of pleasure. This is the philosophy of the Epicureans.

In contrast to the Skeptic view is the philosophy of Epicurus (341–270 B.C.), who founded the school of Epicureanism. Epicurus, like Socrates and Plato, thought that man should strive toward happiness. He also taught that people should not fear death, nor the gods, and should seek pleasure in *this life,* as opposed to seeking austerity in the hopes of earning a pleasant *afterlife.* Because pleasure is the main emphasis of life, Epicureanism is by its nature a hedonistic philosophy, or one that is pleasure-based. However, Epicurus went beyond that simple recommendation to also emphasize the importance of avoiding pleasures that may cause harm in the future. (That's the virtue of temperance.)

MORE PLEASURE, LESS PAIN

Epicurus was harshly critical of other philosophers and philosophies. For example, he thought the Cynics were dangerous and, potentially, enemies of the state. Of his 300 works, only three of his letters survive. These surviving works, however, effectively summarize his philosophy. In them, he linked morality to pleasure, and noted that the goal of life is to minimize pain and maximize pleasure. In *Letter to Menoeceus* he wrote that "pleasure is the beginning and end of the good life. We recognize pleasure as the first good, being natural to us, and it is from pleasure that we begin every choice and avoidance. It is also to pleasure that we return, using it as the standard by which we judge every good."

The difficulty in this approach is figuring out the types of pleasure that lead to human happiness. Epicurus's first step in the quest for a happy and pleasurable life was to eliminate pain as much as possible. He upheld that one major source of fear is religious myth. That fear is experienced when people worry about how gods view them, and if the gods are about to deliver punishment or reward. Epicurus argued that these fears were unfounded. Indeed, we are freed from the fear of the gods because the gods themselves have nothing to do with human affairs. Natural events such as lightning and earthquakes, for example, are entirely the result of the configuration of atoms, and they are not caused by the will of the gods. This is revolutionary thinking for this period of Greek history. Epicurus did not outright deny the existence of the gods, but he did say that they are entirely different than how people commonly imagine them, and that science and faith can live side by side...with some adjustments.

Another fear that leads to pain is the fear of death. Epicurus had a solution for this: He counseled that death need not be feared because the world is wholly material. As such, the soul doesn't survive death, and that, in turn, means a person cannot experience pain after death. Basically, he is saying we should not fear death because there's nothing after death. Cold comfort, but logical.

FINDING THE RIGHT PLEASURES

Epicurus reasoned that to find happiness we must figure out the pleasures that are best for us. We're human, and humans have desires. Some of these desires lead to real happiness, while others lead to pleasure, and then ultimately pain. He described this by breaking down our desires into three levels. The first level of desires are necessary things like basic food and shelter. Pursue those desires, he said. The next level of desires are nicer versions of those basic needs—rich food and big houses, for examples. Epicurus found these problematic because we can't always get them, and if we can't, that will frustrate us. The third level of desires are those that are vain and empty, like wealth, fame, and power. These desires can't be satisfied simply because they are limitless—if we get them, we always want more and will never be happy. These desires should not be pursued, said Epicurus.

Quotable Voices

"Do not spoil what you have by desiring what you have not; remember that what you now have was once among the things you only hoped for." —Epicurus

What's the trick then? Temperance, or pleasure through moderation. Simple pleasures lead to the most happiness and the least pain, while pleasures with an edge will come back to cut you. Take getting drunk, for example. It may be fun, but a hangover and dependency may result.

Temperance leads naturally to happiness because it encourages us to develop virtues, or good habits. Those good habits will lead to good choices in seeking out the best kinds of pleasure that deliver the least amount of pain. Epicurus recommended the usual ancient Greek virtues of courage, honor, justice, and moderation (obviously), but he added another one: prudence, or the ability to make decisions about one's own interests and to act accordingly in a healthy manner.

THE STOICS

Just Be Reasonable

The main gist of Stoic philosophy, or Stoicism, had a huge impact on mainstream moral philosophy. The Stoics believed that reason was the highest authority and that the human ability and gift of reason naturally followed what was natural, or objectively good, and humanity had no need to label it as such. In other words, the Stoics tied our ability to reason with our ability, or even our responsibility, to act in a positive, virtuous, ethical manner.

According to the Stoics, the highest authority at our disposal is reason, which also happens to be a vehicle for the rational laws of nature. However, this makes nature rational. Therefore, we should accept things for the way they are and should not try to change them. Instead, change itself—and ultimately happiness and harmony—can only come from changing the way we act and react. And this change occurs when we rationally analyze and adjust our emotions and actions to get them in sync with nature. The word *stoic*, meaning "unemotional and unaffected," comes from this school of thought. The distinction between the word we use today and the school of thought is subtle but important: a stoic person may not react to an event, whereas a Stoic doesn't see a need to overreact at nature just being nature.

HAPPINESS IN ACCEPTANCE

Stoicism was a tremendously popular philosophy in Hellenistic times, rivaled by its almost opposite, Epicureanism. At the center of

Stoicism is the idea that the universe is by its nature fatalistic. Therefore, the best that humans can do in terms of the pursuit of happiness is just accept it and resign ourselves to this fate, no matter what that individual fate may be. It's depressing for sure, but there's also a freedom in this idea, to admit that there is nothing to be done about the things that one cannot change (which is literally everything outside of our individual selves). Our only option is to accept this reality and move on to other pursuits. If you can't change things, then it would be futile to try, and you would be much happier not doing so. The notion of free will enters into this philosophy, because while we are predestined to do whatever it is we do, we have the choice whether or not to accept this fate—in other words, we can choose to be happy. (Or not.)

Quotable Voices

"Fate is the endless chain of causation, whereby things are; the reason or formula by which the world goes on." —Zeno of Citium

LIVING THE SIMPLE LIFE

The recognized founder of the Stoic school was a philosopher known as Zeno, who was from the city of Citium on the island of Cyprus. His followers were called Zenonians at first but later became referred to as Stoics because Zeno of Citium delivered his lectures to his students on the Painted Porch in the Athens marketplace, an area known as the Stoa Poikile. Zeno lived simply, eating foods that didn't need to be cooked, eschewing wine in favor of water, wearing simple clothes and, like a true stoic, didn't get fazed much by rain, heat, or even physical pain. He lived in this manner because he believed that the most moral way to find happiness was with a denial of pleasure.

One story demonstrates Zeno's philosophy in a very cold way: He once saw a slave being whipped for stealing. The slave said it was his destiny to be a thief. Zeno said it was then also his destiny to get whipped for it. There is a connection, and a consistent one, between our fated destiny and the justice meted out for that behavior. One must accept both. A nonextant text (only references of it survive) called *Republic* notes that Zeno advocated for the abolishment of civil institutions, including money, temples, law courts, and marriage. He also thought genders should dress alike from head to toe and also practice free love. All of this, he believed, were constraints that held us down, and abolishing them would free us to live much simpler lives.

Three Parts

Zeno broke philosophy into the area of logic, physics, and ethics. In his lectures he compared these areas to an animal, making up a whole out of necessary, interconnected parts: logic is the bones and sinew, physics is flesh, and ethics was the soul.

Even though Zeno disliked the institutions that directed moral behavior through punishments and rules, he believed that we should adopt virtues, for these were natural and part of our nature. Zeno advocated following the laws, for they were based on the principles of the cosmos. He thought laws of society reflected the order that nature so carefully created by itself. It was up to us to use our human reasoning skills to find those parallel rational laws in society, and ourselves.

PLOTINUS AND NEOPLATONISM

All That's Old Is New Again

Neoplatonism was the fifth new school of ethics that followed in the wake of Socrates, Plato, and Aristotle. As you might suspect, there are some similarities between Neoplatonism and Platonism, with the "neo" suggesting a new form, or a revival of Platonic thought. Indeed, the Neoplatonists of the time considered themselves followers of Plato and his philosophies. The adherents of this movement, which was founded in the third century A.D., just called themselves Platonists. But their theories were different enough from what Plato and Aristotle had put forth that the Neoplatonism label was applied by the nineteenth century.

Quotable Voices

"Being is desirable because it is identical with Beauty, and Beauty is loved because it is Being. We ourselves possess Beauty when we are true to our own being; ugliness is in going over to another order; knowing ourselves, we are beautiful; in self-ignorance, we are ugly." —Plotinus

The founder of Neoplatonism was an Egyptian philosopher named Plotinus (ca. A.D. 204–270). He honed his theories while he lived in Alexandria (then under tremendous Greek influence), and then Rome. He was influenced by classical philosophers, like Plato of course, along with some Persian and Indian philosophies he picked up in his travels, along with some native Egyptian theological principles. All he intended to do was preserve and spread and modernize the teachings of Plato (and Socrates by extension), but he wound up fusing Platonic ideas with a bit of Asian and Middle Eastern mysticism. At age forty Plotinus established his own school, where he taught in a conversational, informal style and wrote fifty-four treatises, later collected into a single work (by his ambitious student Porphyry) called *Enneads*.

BACK TO ONE

Neoplatonism has more religious elements than does Platonism. Plotinus was fascinated with the abstract, physical forms of concepts. From that he created a metaphysical model of the universe. He held that there is somewhere a single source, called the One, from which all reality and all of existence radiates. (Also called the Good, or Absolute, Plotinus said it has "its center everywhere but its circumference nowhere.") As objects move further out from this center of pure goodness and immortality, they lose levels of beauty and thus divinity. This means that those things on the far outskirts from this central point become corrupted and have very little of that goodness left—such as the human soul. Evil, then, is merely the absence of good, which comes from the act of sin, and it is committed by beings lost and disconnected from the One.

The ethical path therefore, as Plotinus asserted, was the one that gets people back to the One. That path begins with careful examination of the world and everything in it. That leads to an understanding and appreciation of innate goodness, which in turn leads to examination and understanding of larger and more complicated objects and concepts. Eventually, that brings the individual to finally contemplate the One, and achieve an understanding of all of the knowledge of nature. This makes philosophical activity a wholesome, healing experience. To reflect and study doesn't just answer questions about the universe, it actually brings a person closer into it, and closer to the goodness and truth at its core.

The more united a person is with this mystical force, the more rewards and true virtues that person acquires. In Neoplatonism, those virtues are the same cardinal virtues as in Plato: justice, prudence, temperance, and courage. These values, in turn, help a person on the path to the One, as well as to achieve the ideal of eudaimonia, or ultimate happiness.

Chapter 3

CONSEQUENTIALIST ETHICS

Consequentialism is one of the main ethical theories of the past few hundred years. Very generally put, it stresses that the focus of an ethical matter and its ethical weight resides on the person, or agent, by way of that person's actions or consequences. In other words, this focus and weight lead to quantifiably useful or generally positive ends, such as the well-being of humans and animals.

There are a few different kinds of consequentialism. One of them is found in the broad school of thought called utilitarianism. Very generally put, utilitarianism states that morality is about maximizing the most pleasure and minimizing the most pain as much as possible. A utilitarian is someone who believes that it's important to act in an ethical fashion to spread happiness, relieve suffering, create freedom, or help humanity thrive and survive, or any one of these notions. Further, that person feels a moral obligation to do so, and that the outcome is always more important than the intent.

Another type of consequentialist moral philosophy is rule consequentialism, also called rule utilitarianism. Rule consequentialism follows all the same ideas of consequentialism, but with a backbone or framework of a legal system or ethical code. For example, the right action among several choices has been laid out within the ethical system already, and therefore has been accepted as a moral truth by the community, because it provides the best possible outcome. This is seen a lot in lawmaking and law enforcement. For example, a community may think it is moral to make bank robbers perform community service work because it helps the community—that is, this service work provides a societal benefit beyond just a jail sentence.

In opposition to rule utilitarianism is the bit more theoretical, less practical, and more pensive style of consequentialist moral philosophy called act utilitarianism. In this school, an agent's moral action is right if, and only if, it produces at least as much happiness as another choice that the agent could have chosen. This one is a bit more subjective, because how does one weigh out the happiness of theoretical actions?

There's also the matter of ethical altruism. Like other kinds of utilitarianism, ethical altruism is consequence-minded and -oriented. This philosophy judges that the best moral acts are the ones that lead to the most happiness for others—but only others. Happiness comes at the detriment of the agent, and this is the most moral act possible. It's all about the happiness of others at the complete and total sacrifice of one's own happiness.

Of course, each of these aspects of consequentialism have pros and cons, so let's discuss them further in the coming pages.

NORMATIVE ETHICS AND DESCRIPTIVE ETHICS

Thinking Right versus Acting Right

Any discussion or study of ethics can be split into two essential but different questions: "Why?" and "How?"

Investigations into "why" humans act cover the guiding, underlying principles of ethical standards such as virtue, human behavior, fear of consequence, and desire for happiness. This aspect of ethics is also called *normative ethics*, and it is concerned with figuring out the meat of morality. The end goal of normative ethics is to help us determine the proper course of action for human behavior, which is to say the most moral, correct, or just ways of thinking and acting. One basic example of normative ethics is Immanuel Kant's Categorical Imperative. It states that morality is an outgrowth of rational thought, and it's normative because it seeks to define the best way a person *should* act.

"How" humans actually act, whether in adhering to a standard moral code or not, is a completely different situation altogether. Have you ever heard a parent say to their child, "Do as I say, not as I do?" This quip exposes the major difference between theory and action, or "ought to" and "actually does." Ethics define us as humans, but the disconnect between having a sense of what is morally good and doing another thing anyway may more accurately define us as humans.

The actions that result (or do not result) from normative ethics fall under the banner of *descriptive ethics*. John Stuart Mill's principle of utility is a kind of descriptive ethics. It's an examination of behavior itself, as opposed to the ethics that lead to behavior, and defines good actions as ones that promote happiness or pleasure. To make a long story short: Ideals and ideas are normative ethical theories, and actual actions (and the process that surrounds them) are descriptive ethics.

JUST SOME REGULAR, NORMATIVE ETHICS

Normative ethical theories are any ethical theories that debate the innate or natural value of an action, thought, or feeling—particularly if it is objectively right or wrong. Determining virtues and their reach is a normative ethical practice. So is debating the rightness or wrongness of actions based on their consequences—yes, action is ultimately involved but in terms of normative ethics the practice is more about the motivating factors behind the action, and not the action itself.

Here are some normative ethical quandaries:

- If killing is accepted as being wrong, is it morally acceptable to put convicted murderers to death?
- Is it morally acceptable to free slaves because the practice is abhorrent, even though freeing them would violate the laws of a community that permits it?
- Is there ever an acceptable reason to inflict pain upon another person?

In many ways, normative ethics is like high-level etiquette. They are wrapped up in the manners of life, and how people ought to behave toward one another so as not to offend. But it's way more complex than that. Ethics are of major importance and override the rules and laws of society, and are often a matter of life and death, and as some ethicists would argue, describe the pursuit of happiness. While it is morally acceptable and encouraged to be polite, normative ethics frame our ability to live our lives in a just and free manner.

BE MORE DESCRIPTIVE

Descriptive ethics, then, are all about action—how those normative ethics are used where it really counts. It's the study of how human beings actually behave in the ethical realm, whether they're actively considering the ethical ramifications of their actions or not. Descriptive ethics is what humans do to one another and themselves—the "applied" in applied ethics. (This may be an easier term to understand than descriptive ethics, and the term *applied ethics* is used just as often, if not more so, than descriptive ethics.) It's a little confusing, but descriptive ethics also concern the motivations of social behavior, such as how people reason their way through ethics, what people consider to be the most important factors in action, and the regulation of behavior based on those standards on a society- or community-wide level. Recall that normative ethics are all about the theories of *why*, whereas descriptive ethics are all about understanding the actions of *how*.

Descriptive ethics is just as rooted in sciences like psychology, anthropology, and sociology as it is philosophy. One example of descriptive ethics is how widely acceptable moral standards are used to form laws. For example, the actions that a society chooses to punish its members is an insight into the ethics of the people of that society.

"At the descriptive level, certainly, you would expect different cultures to develop different sorts of ethics and obviously they have; that doesn't mean that you can't think of overarching ethical principles you would want people to follow in all kinds of places." —Twentieth-century Australian ethicist Peter Singer

One other important, elementary force in ethics is the concept of metaethics. This is really what the overarching study of ethics is about. In trying to determine how to act and why via normative and descriptive ethical forms, metaethics seeks to investigate the source of the ethical principles that make us choose one course of action over another. This is where things like divine intervention, universal truths, and reason come into play—the soil from which all other ethical philosophies grow.

JEREMY BENTHAM AND MEASURING UTILITY

Happiness Through Calculus

Utilitarianism is the most dominant and the easiest to understand of the major consequentialist theories. At its most basic level, utilitarianism states that if one can increase the overall happiness of the world, or that of an individual, or just make the world a better place, then one should. In fact, one has a moral obligation to do so. The pursuit of happiness is the thing that separates utilitarianism, as set forth by British philosopher Jeremy Bentham (1748–1832), from other forms of consequentialism.

This makes utilitarianism a relatively sunny and easy-to-get-behind ethical theory. After all, everybody wants happiness or enlightenment or peace. But it's actually a quite complicated theory to apply to daily life. Because outcomes or consequences are based on happiness, utilitarians are tasked with making predictions, judgments, or claims about what they think makes any one consequence good or bad. Even though the end goal is maximum happiness, acting in a utilitarian way requires impartiality. You're after overall, "universal" happiness, not necessarily the thing that feels the best or nicest in that moment for you or the other person you're interacting with.

BENTHAM'S SLIDING SCALE

Jeremy Bentham was the first Western philosopher to write extensively about utilitarianism. In his 1789 book *An Introduction to the*

Principles of Morals and Legislation, Bentham explained that the way to judge consequences on that sliding but definitive scale of "good" and "bad" is the amount of happiness, pleasure, or benefit they'll lead to for one person, and then weigh those consequences against the amount of pain, suffering, and struggle it might cause another. Unfortunately, life is rarely so black and white. In any number of examples, one person might get great benefit at a great cost to another. But, Bentham argues, one can try to work out and reason through this problem by way of qualitative values. If the hurt person gets more pain than the pleasure the pleased person got, then it's not a morally good decision. If the winner got more pleasure out of the action and the loser just got a little inconvenienced or miffed, then it is a moral decision, because there was an overall benefit, all things considered. This is where impartiality comes into play—difficult as it may be, one must decide with utility in mind, and kind of ignore the individual feelings of the people whom the decision would affect.

Quotable Voices

"The said truth is that it is the greatest happiness of the greatest number that is the measure of right and wrong." —Jeremy Bentham

Bentham defined the goods of happiness and pleasure, and the absence of pain and suffering, as his core thesis: He called it the principle of utility. Utility is about purpose and use, and there is usually little emotional meaning attached to the word *utility*. It just means "the thing that works best is the best thing." Bentham, however, called "pleasure" utility because he put it in such high esteem. At its essence, utilitarianism is a theory in which good or moral consequences, and thus moral actions, are defined in terms of an end result that leads to as much good as possible and as little bad as possible...or at least more good than bad. The goal: shoot for 51 percent or higher on the "good" side of an issue.

THE ETHICAL ALGORITHM

It's in analyzing and weighing consequences that Bentham made his most lasting contribution to moral philosophy. For example, the different consequences from an action can, and most often will be, notably different from each other. It's hard to argue that a good intention matters the most in a moral decision when the theoretical good of that intention leads to a quantifiably bad or misery-causing outcome. And so, to fine-tune his argument that consequences can and should be measured as scientifically and logically as possible, he developed a moral algorithm called Utility Calculus, or Hedonism Calculus. (While it's not the same theory as Voltaire's notion of pleasure-seeking-is-the-one-true-way hedonism, Bentham does advocate the pursuit and maximization of pleasure, which is the entire point of hedonism, and so the name does seem appropriate.) With his system, Bentham quantifies the moral aspects of actions in this way: The greater the good of an action, the more "hedons" or "positive utility units" it's worth.

- **Intensity.** What is the intensity or level or pleasure and/or pain that the action leads to?
- **Duration.** What is the duration of that pleasure or pain the action creates?

- **Certainty.** Is there a notable amount of certainty or uncertainty of pleasure or pain resulting from the action?
- **Propinquity.** How soon after the action does the pleasure or pain kick in? Is it near or far? For example, the benefits of eating healthy take a while for the benefit to kick in, in the form of a lower cholesterol level over time. But eating a cheeseburger? The pleasure is immediate.
- **Fecundity.** How likely is the action to be followed by even more pleasure (if it's a pleasurable act) or pain (if it's not so pleasurable)?
- **Purity.** How pure or impure is the pleasure or pain after an action? As an opposite of the previous metric, this asks how likely the feeling after an action is to be followed by the exact opposite.
- **Extent.** What is the extent of the effect of the action?

Can you imagine going through this process multiple times a day to make a decision to see if it's moral or not? Using Bentham's system of determination requires slow, deliberate action. Ethics isn't easy! But Bentham didn't really mean for it to be used for every decision to be made, but only for troubling decisions and for big political or public policy decisions.

JOHN STUART MILL AND UTILITARIANISM

Utility Player

British philosopher John Stuart Mill (1806–1873) expounded on Jeremy Bentham's establishment of utilitarianism. While he agreed with the philosophy's central concept that the definition of a good moral act was one that boasted the maximum utility, which is to say as much pleasure and as little pain as possible, he had a big problem with the way Bentham defined pleasure and pain. Mill stressed that "pleasure" and "pain" cannot be quantified, even with Bentham's Hedonism Calculus, because pleasure and pain are incredibly subjective. Each person has a different idea of what pleasure and pain means to him, and how he measures them. Have you ever been asked to rate your level of pain at the hospital? That rating uses a 1 to 10 scale. But those numbers are relative to…what? That's the problem with Bentham's plan, Mill argued: it's too subjective. Even one person's definition of pleasure and pain may change from one day to the next, or from one specific situation to the next.

RELATIVE PLEASURE

It's as simple as a matter of taste. Millions of people derive great pleasure from watching reality TV, while others may find it trashy. One person may find the height of pleasure in the enjoyment of a $200 bottle of wine, whereas a person who prefers sweet drinks might find the wine awful tasting. One isn't better than the other—it's just a matter of preference. And some people like both. Mill doesn't think we should compare them. All are legitimate sources of pleasure—comparison just complicates the reasoning behind utilitarian analysis.

Groomed

John Stuart Mill's father, James Mill, was also a utilitarian philosopher and a friend of Jeremy Bentham. Together they explicitly set out to mold John Stuart Mill into a defender and writer of utilitarianism.

Some pleasures, as far as Mill is concerned, are actually greater than others. These higher pleasures are something like virtues. If the pleasures are associated with reason, deliberation, or other emotions that lead to social change and benefit, then they are of a higher pleasure. These are intellectual and spiritual pleasures. Failing that, the pleasure is merely in the realm of the other earthly delights—what Mill called "sensations." This is what shields utilitarianism from the criticism that haunts hedonism. (Mill called hedonism a "doctrine only worthy of a swine.") Mill's utilitarianism is pleasure seeking with a purpose—pleasure seeking for the greater good—which makes life about more than just an existence of pleasure seeking. To that end, pleasure and goodness mean the greater good, and not just feeling good individually. Such pleasures are of higher moral value because they lead to the greater overall good, as well as the individual good. Some utilitarians find their support for the pursuit of happiness in God's will, or in divine command theory. More hedonistic, pleasure/pain-regulating utilitarians like Mill argue for a happiness based on the mind and body because the physical human experience is quantifiable, provable, and immediate.

THE NEED FOR PLEASURE

John Stuart Mill wasn't one to go around trying to "prove" a theory that was all about subjectivity. In his book *Utilitarianism*, for example, he writes about proving the principle of utility in terms of the overwhelmingly universal human need and pursuit for happiness. To him, this need is just as real as seeing an object, or hearing a sound. Because this need so obviously exists, there's no need for him to prove that it is real. That happiness pursuit unites us, he suggests, and if we're all pursuing happiness, then it leads to overall greater happiness for all.

Quotable Voices

"The only proof capable of being given that an object is visible, is that people actually see it. The only proof that a sound is audible, is that people hear it. In like manner, I apprehend, the sole evidence it is possible to produce that anything is desirable, is that people do actually desire it....No reason can be given why the general happiness is desirable, except that each person, so far as he believes it to be attainable, desires his own happiness....[W]e have not only all the proof which the case admits of, but all which it is possible to require, that happiness is a good: that each person's happiness is a good to that person, and the general happiness, therefore, a good to the aggregate of all persons." —John Stuart Mill

Pleasure, to Mill, is a goal worth pursuing in and of itself. It doesn't have to be a nice byproduct of acting morally, or the only reason to do things. Pleasure is moral, and morality is pleasure. This can be applied to religion as well, as religion and ethical study help people find pleasure and happiness and avoid emotional pain. But it's also okay to pursue those goals independently of any other construct. In this regard, ethics is just about adding happiness to the world...or at the very least, minimizing pain.

As far as Bentham and Mill are concerned, they are of the utilitarian mind-set that everyone's happiness and/or pain matter. They are, of course, utilitarian, and as such they are always trying to decide what is the best, or the most useful, course of action. Taking into account how more than one party would be affected by a moral decision is a big part of what utilitarians do. It's all about the net gain of utility. They don't care who gains, just as long as gain is there in some way. This is called "an equal consideration of interests."

ETHICAL ALTRUISM

Be Excellent to Each Other

A lot of ethical principles are, for lack of a better word, self-absorbed. Many seem to ask some variation of the questions, "How can *I* live a better life?" "Am *I* doing the right things?" "Does *my* ability to reason determine whether or not I make an ethical decision?" Those questions are indeed important to ask in the study and in the practice of ethics. But enough about me—what about other people?

In altruism, the good of others is the rightful end of a moral action. Specifically, an action is morally right only if the result or consequences of the action are more favorable than not to anyone and everyone *except* the agent. The good of others is the true and rightful end, then, of any moral action.

STAYING POSITIVE

French philosopher Auguste Comte (1798–1857) was the founder of positivism, a doctrine that was the opposite of egoism, or the idea to pursue one's self interests above all others. Whereas egoism dictates that humans operate out of their own best interests, Comte believed that humans should act for the good of others. He described the ethical doctrines behind positivism with the phrase "live for others," as well as a term he coined, *altruism*. In fact, altruism comes from the word *alter*, which in Latin means "other," and so a good name for this philosophy could be "otherism." Comte and other altruists believe that a moral agent (a person) has the obligation to further the pleasures and resolve the pain of others.

"The only real life is the collective life of the race; individual life has no existence except as an abstraction." —Auguste Comte

ALL FOR YOU

Ethics are, of course, innately about how one individual treats another—and if that treatment is as absolutely and objectively morally "good" as possible. But the doctrine of ethical altruism is almost completely about the consequences of actions and the resulting happiness of somebody else—the effect on the individual doesn't matter much at all. (Except how, by doing one's moral due diligence in a completely selfless way, the agent benefits in the way that being a morally good person is beneficial.) Ethical altruism qualifies as a utilitarian method of ethical practice because it focuses on the outcome of actions, not the intentions behind the actions.

It's all about living to strive for the happiness of others rather than one's own or—as some of the more extreme adherents would argue—at the *expense* of one's own happiness or general well-being. Even regular ethical altruism is radical because it rejects the value of the self as a form of helping others. After all, if you're worried about your own happiness, you can't be truly devoted to helping others— and helping others is what makes a person morally right. In general terms, altruism means to help someone out of generosity, or because it's a nice thing to do, and expecting nothing in return. Such actions are an "everyday" version of altruism.

PROBLEMS WITH ETHICAL ALTRUISM

There are some flaws to the theory. For example, critics have brought up the argument that altruism considers the happiness of others to be the ultimate end, but altruism completely dismisses the idea of individual, self-created, or self-directed happiness. Therein lies the problem: if there's no moral imperative to create happiness for yourself, why should anyone else be inclined to promote your happiness?

There's also the happiness subjectivity problem. The moral agent is the one in charge of the happiness of another—but should he be? Does he have the right to determine and act for someone else's happiness? Acting on behalf of someone else's humanity and happiness is theoretically good, but in practice the idea falls apart if the agent and beneficiary don't see eye to eye on how to help. For example, a rich man sees a poor man shivering on the street in the dead of winter. The rich man gives the poor man his coat. This is certainly an act of altruism, and a utilitarian one because it has the outcome in mind, specifically, the act of helping someone else. But maybe that coatless man didn't need a coat. Maybe he just left his coat inside, and the building was locked, and he's waiting to go back in. Or perhaps the coat is a leather jacket, and the shivering man objects to the killing of animals.

One other major critic of altruism was Ayn Rand (1905–1982), the Russian-American novelist and originator of the objectivist school of political theory that advocated self-sufficiency. She held that altruism was responsible for more harm than good, arguing that there is no rational reason or proof for why sacrificing oneself is morally better than pursuing one's own interest.

RULE CONSEQUENTIALISM

This Theory Rules

Act consequentialism is a direct approach to maximizing utility, or using reasoning to decide your way into actions with morally just consequences. Ultimately (and hopefully) these actions will create more bad than good. But there is more than one way to approach consequence-based ethics with the goal of utility in mind. There's also the indirect approach, or more formally and descriptively, rule consequentialism. In act consequentialism (the direct form of utilitarianism), great attention and effort must be paid to directly maximizing the "good" out of a specific decision-making situation. Rule consequentialism is different—the focus, generally speaking, revolves around examining the results of what happens when people act according to a system of laws, codes, or rules.

MAXIMIZING HAPPINESS

Rule consequentialism forces the moral agent to examine the innate goodness or badness of certain rules generally thought to be good or bad when that person makes a decision. In other words, doing something bad can sometimes be something good…if it leads to maximized happiness in the consequences. Take the example of the white lie, or the lie that is done to save someone's hurt feelings:

"Does my new haircut make me look cool?"

Now, all considerations and situations aside, most ethicists—and most people, really—will say that lying is generally and usually wrong. It is not virtuous to be deceptive, and the truth is pure and good. Getting to the truth is the overarching point of ethics and philosophy anyhow. But from a rule consequentialist point of view, it's not necessarily bad. In some situations, telling the truth can maximize utility and also be a virtuous act. And that act, in and of itself, builds utility, or is something that it's assumed a "good person" would do. But rule consequentialism is explicitly about the situation. It's like that phrase "read the room." Rule consequentialists "read the room" of a situation on a case-by-case basis so that they may determine what is the best possible option to maximize utility in that situation. Depending on the situation, a usually "moral" act like telling the truth might not be the best option.

Back to the example, let's say it's your opinion that the new haircut does not make your friend look cool. It makes him look bald, or old, or something else that he doesn't want to be perceived as, and it would hurt his feelings if you were to tell him as much. Even though your opinion is subjective, the pain and hurt he would feel is definitely real, and you should assume this. The right thing to do, in this case, would be to lie and say, "You look great." Why? Even though you've lied, you've maximized utility by making your friend happy and you've eliminated the potential for pain, as is your moral obligation. Furthermore, your approach was indirect. You didn't directly look at the good or bad of the consequences, but instead weighed how a "bad" act like lying might indirectly lead to a "good" thing, like confidence. This scenario describes rule consequentialism because it both examines and applies the effects and consequences of an oft-used rule or code.

FOLLOWING THE STEPS

A series of precise mental steps can be used to ascertain how to read a situation so as to come up with the best possible outcome from all the outcomes, with a focus on how a certain handling of long-held rules can maximize utility in the consequences.

Quotable Voices

"Capacity for the nobler feelings is in most natures a very tender plant, easily killed, not only by hostile influences, but by mere want of sustenance; and in the majority of young persons it speedily dies away if the occupations to which their position in life has devoted them, and the society into which it has thrown them, are not favorable to keeping that higher capacity in exercise."
—John Stuart Mill

This mental process involves looking at the big picture of a decision. After all, this is rule consequentialism, and so a rule has to be taken to task before it can be acted upon. Going back to the example of the haircut, this mental process involves these steps:

- Ask yourself what the world would look like, hypothetically, if everyone were to take on what you did as a rule. For example, lying to protect someone's feelings. Are you okay if this became a universally agreed upon positive behavior? If so, it's moral.
- Then ask yourself what the world would look like (again, you're considering the consequences) if everybody did the opposite. For example, it would be okay to tell the truth all the time no matter what, because lying is inherently wrong. In all likelihood

people would get upset a lot more often. Would you be okay with *always* telling the truth regardless of situation if that became a universally agreed upon positive behavior? If so, is this the moral choice?

- Then, looking at the two options, you must choose the option that would lead to the best consequences in terms of happiness.

ACT CONSEQUENTIALISM

It's All Just an Act

What really matters in consequentialism are the results of your actions—the consequences, in other words. Utilitarians, then, think that what really matters about those consequences—by which we mean what is good and what is bad—is the amount of utility innate in those consequences. The more utility, or usefulness, or happiness, or goodness, and the less pain and suffering, the better.

But that's a very general view. Because when dealing with happiness and suffering as a result of actions, it's important to look at the who, not just the what. Whose happiness and suffering are we talking about here? The victim? The moral agent? All people? And are all equal?

In consequentialist ethics, the general way to live the right and good way is by seeking to maximize the good (and thus pleasure, in some abstract way, for someone) via ethical, moral actions. But how does one do that? One major strategy for doing that is called act consequentialism. It's a very direct approach. In act consequentialism, both the consequences of an action and the people who would be impacted by the action matter. The goal is not to choose just the option that produces the most overall happiness, statistically speaking, but the option that offers up the best consequences, within that situation, for the people involved. Which people? All the people.

CHOOSING HOW TO ACT

Because act consequentialism is about both the outcome as well as the people involved, this ethical approach tends to create situations that have emotional resonance. By its nature, because compassion and thinking about others is involved, act consequentialism is not impartial like the other forms of utilitarianism or consequentialism. But in order to determine which action is the one best for people, a series of procedures, in order, have to be logically and carefully worked through.

First, you must determine all of the possible options so that you can see all of your choices in front of you and compare and contrast them. This way, you will see which produces the maximum amount of good, or utility. Let's take an example: As you're driving to work, you see a dog lying in the road, evidently hit by a driver who took off. Nobody else has stopped to help, and the dog is injured, bleeding, and breathing heavily. Making matters worse, your phone is dead, so you can't just call the authorities or animal control and let others solve the problem for you. It's fallen on you to take time out of your day, get the dog to an animal hospital, and quickly. That is, if you choose to help.

FORMULATING THE DECISION

So, what options do you have? In a bare bones, black-and-white sort of way, there are two possibilities immediately open to you. You can choose:

- Option 1. Pull over, try to pick up the dog, put her in your car, and drive her to the nearest animal hospital.
- Option 2. Just keep driving, ignore the animal, and arrive at work on time.

How do you make this choice? First you must determine the "direct calculations" regarding the relative levels of possible good outcomes. These calculations are questions you can answer to the best of your ability, such as: Who will receive the most benefit from each decision? Who will get the most discomfort from each? In this case, you might look at it in terms of the characters involved: you and the dog.

In the first option, you are immediately impacted in a negative way. This isn't to say it's a painful or bad impact, only that it's objectively negative. You'll have to get out of a car on a busy road, try to get an injured dog into your car, get it to a hospital, pay the bill, and probably be late for work and upset your boss and coworkers. So those people are indirectly affected as well, and their involvement should not be discounted or ignored.

The dog, however, benefits greatly. In danger of dying a painful death, the literal physical pain she feels could be over as soon as you get her to a hospital. Once there, she will receive medical care and medicine and hopefully make a full recovery.

Quotable Voices

In his 2016 novella *The Four Thousand, the Eight Hundred,* Australian science-fiction writer Greg Egan touched on a problem with making decisions based on maximizing the good: "We have a special name, here, for a certain kind of failure to defer to the greater good—for putting a personal sense of doing right above any objective measure of the outcome. It's called 'moral vanity.'"

Take now the second option. You get to work on time, and your boss and coworkers see you walk in the door and they know they can count on you. That you showed up for work on time is a benefit to them, and it's a benefit to you in that your coworkers trust you. But you also failed to help out an injured animal when you could have done so. You didn't increase happiness and decrease pain when you readily could have, which is a violation of the utilitarian ethical code. After all, as far as you know the dog continues to lie in the street, slowly dying from painful injuries.

This raises the question: can you measure the relative amounts of pleasure and pain generated by the given set of options? Act consequentialists say that you can, with something called positive utility units, or hedons. The more good an action, and more "hedons" it's worth. (This system was devised by utilitarian pioneer Jeremy Bentham in his 1789 book, *An Introduction to the Principles of Morals and Legislation*.) How many positive utility units should you offer for each thing? Once you figure that out, says the theory, then it's time to choose the right option. It's a numbers game—pick the choice with the higher number of positive utility units.

CRITICISMS OF CONSEQUENTIALIST ETHICS

There Will Be Consequences

There are so many different general theories of moral philosophy—and variations within those general theories—for a reason. Let's be honest here: While the progenitors of each theory may disagree, none of the theories provides a 100 percent perfect way to approach the difficult decisions of life. Also, this is a subjective area: one theory may feel more right than others, or one may feel like the better approach based on the circumstance.

To that end, although consequentialism provides a solid ethical framework, in that it considers the consequences and the people involved in the ethics of decision-making above all other things, there are some prominent critics of the theory who have pointed out some flaws within the system.

NONSENSE ON STILTS

One problem with consequentialism can be predicted in the words of utilitarian pioneer Jeremy Bentham himself. He once likened the notion of social justice to "nonsense on stilts." Indeed, one could say that personal rights and justice are not as important in consequentialism as they are in other philosophical schools. This is because consequentialism favors, well, the best consequences. Sometimes a subjective or emotional issue like justice or rights don't factor into the simple math of a system that favors not the greater good but literally "the most good." It assumes, for example, the two parties in a situation are equal. If party A loses money and party B gains money due to a decision, in theory that outcome is good enough for a consequentialist. But what if party A is broke and starving and has to pay an unfair tax to party B, who has plenty to go around and is furthermore exploiting an unfair tax law in the system? As long as the suffering of one is outweighed by the happiness of another—regardless of who they are—then it's morally fine.

Oddly enough, this outcome just feels wrong. This is because it plays to our sense of decency and justice, which some moral philosophers would argue is what makes us human. Ignoring these feelings for the sake of following the theory to the letter is precisely what led philosophers to spin off the direct approach into the indirect approach. We must weigh many factors when making any decision.

THE PROBLEM WITH IDEALISM

Another difficulty about utilitarianism is that, and this is despite the aforementioned flaw, it's far too idealistic to use all the time. It requires adherents to exercise utility almost constantly—because it is of extreme moral importance to always make the decisions that maximize good and eliminate pain. It's simply unrealistic to expect people to constantly and thoroughly analyze every decision they make in terms of how it affects the big picture, and who it affects. For most people, common sense and common decency are enough of a moral compass—they don't need to and they certainly don't want to involve a complex and often arbitrary mathematical process into the hundreds of decisions they make each day. We know that people suffer, and most of us don't want to add to the suffering, especially when faced with it head-on. Moral philosophy and ethics are indeed about the big picture, but utilitarianism could be said to be a little too obsessed with the minutia.

Quotable Voices

"The majority of philosophers are totally humorless. That's part of their trouble."
—Bernard Williams

WHERE IS THE INDIVIDUAL?

Utilitarianism can be so overwhelmingly specific, especially when trying to make it a system of second nature thoughts and analyses, that it can separate people from their true ethical natures. Philosopher Bernard Williams (1929–2003) argued that the consequentialist theory of utilitarianism robs people of their unique, individual moral outlooks by making them follow a finite and narrow system; and to do so is to rob people of their independence, reasoning skills, and other things that make them inherently human. If you think about it, this means utilitarianism is really a method for causing pain instead of happiness, because it robs people of their basic humanity. In other words, there's not as much utility in utilitarianism.

Williams explained his idea with an ethical conundrum. A man named George is an unemployed scientist, a situation based in part of his refusal to ever use his skills and experience to work for a company or government that makes biological weapons. One day he hears about a lucrative, interesting job working for a government laboratory making a new kind of biochemical weapon. Even though he's unemployed, he still resists in taking the job. However, he is pursued for the job, as is another biochemist named Greg. If George refuses, Greg will take it—and will work one hundred hours a week, day and night, because he's both a workhorse and actually has a fervent desire to make the weapons to destroy his country's enemies, whoever they may be. That's the ethical dilemma for George: if he did take the job, against his moral code, he could purposely work slowly, making as few weapons as possible, and maybe a lot of duds, thus minimizing the number of lives lost as compared to Greg who, if he took the job, would make a lot more working weapons. But George, remember, is against making weapons.

Williams argues that utilitarianism would say that George should take the job because it leads to the best possible outcome: he gets a job, and fewer people die. But isn't it bad that George has to betray his core beliefs and identity? Must he abandon everything for a job, and for the blind adherence to a moral theory?

NOT YOUR PLACE

Utilitarianism contains another interesting flaw. To suggest that people can truly have a full understanding of exactly how (and how much) their decisions will affect the happiness of others, and thus produce the most good, is an arrogant notion. No one can truly know which decision they make will ultimately produce the most good. Because utilitarianism demands the mathematical calculations to make predictions—and assumes those predicted outcomes are the exact outcomes of what would happen—the whole process is a gross exercise in egoism and wishful thinking.

Chapter 4

DEONTOLOGICAL ETHICS

Western philosophy came from the ancient Greeks, and one of the dominant forms of moral philosophy comes from the Greek language itself. *Deon* is the Greek word for duty. From that word comes the ethical concept of deontology. Deontology holds that morality is based on duties and obligations—that we as humans are bound by some unwritten code or codified system to do and say the objectively right thing.

Another major tenet of deontological ethical theories is the idea that some actions simply seem or feel right, and they are adopted far and wide as such because they intrinsically are right. These actions are objectively and morally good, and they would have these qualities even without humans to come along and say as much. There's a reason why certain good and moral attributes, such as courage and honesty, have been championed by cultures all over the world. More important, actions of courage and honesty are right in themselves—regardless of the consequences that arise from doing those things. But because the moral agents—people—choose to act on that objectively morally correct truth, they are doing the morally correct thing. Even if their action leads to unhappiness, their hands are clean because they acted with the purest of intentions and from a very pure place.

Using deontological ethical theories, it's difficult to examine the moral validity of an action without taking its consideration into account (because that would be consequentialism), but deontology is a fascinating theory that puts the moral responsibility not on the agent but back onto the universe, which is ultimately blameless and unpunishable. Take this example: A child runs away from home because his parents are abusive, and he seeks comfort at the home of his uncle, a deontologist. This deontologist uncle may believe that abusing one's child is inherently wrong, but that same uncle may also believe that it is morally correct to reunite the child with his parents. Knowing full well that the child will likely be abused again, the uncle sends the child home, fully confident that his actions were moral, because the action in and of itself, without any other things considered, is the right thing to do from an extremely objective stance.

Another example of deontological ethical theory involves the obligation factor. This aspect of deontology is especially intriguing when the consequences of an action may result in personal harm, or at least decreased benefit. We all know that parents are obligated to take care of their children. The deontological view says that parents are morally correct to fulfill that obligation, even though doing so may bring them decreased pleasure. (Taking care of children takes time and money, and the parent will have less of those.) Although many ethical theories take consequences and the effect of personal happiness into consideration, for deontologists the sake of fulfilling innate moral obligations takes precedent. Some actions just can't be justified by the results. Deontology upends old aphorisms: the road *away from* hell is paved with good intentions; and the ends *do not* justify the means.

In this chapter, we'll explore the finer points (and flaws) of some of the major ideas in deontology. Among them are the major deontological mind of Immanuel Kant and his Categorical Imperative, which is an intricate, thought-guiding process that can help people determine if an action is moral, and John Rawls, a twentieth-century deontologist who used the deontological ideas of innately moral actions to advocate for a more just and fair political system.

IMMANUEL KANT AND KANTIANISM

Rules Are Meant to Be Followed

The moral theory of utilitarianism argues that people have an ethical obligation to take the course of action that will lead to the most positive outcome. (And the best outcome is happiness, because that's the absolute best possibility.) Consequentialism dictates that humans consider any possible outcome of an action, be it "good" or "bad," especially because the outcome of that act would reveal the act itself to be objectively morally "right" or "wrong." In the moral philosophy of deontology, by contrast, outcomes and consequences are not as important in the decision-making process, or in the evaluation of right versus wrong. In this philosophy, it's about the moral nature of the overriding rules and principles that guide the act. Acting under a morally correct rule system guarantees that doing the right thing is the right thing, regardless of the outcome or consequences.

In terms of religion, deontology is a big deal. Most any major religion's tenets derive from a set of divine commands, or commandments, that make adherents morally obligated not to engage in clearly defined immoral acts. In Christianity, for example, lying, stealing, and laying with thy neighbor's wife are objectively immoral acts because the moral system set forth by the Ten Commandments explicitly says that they are.

These religious moral ideas can be used outside of a religious system, a concept called secular deontological moral theory. The most cohesive, thorough, and lasting writings on the ideas were set forth by Immanuel Kant (1724–1804) in the late 1700s. Rather than deriving some kind of universal or widely accepted moral code from divine rules, church laws, or maxims, Kant's theory of deontology comes from what he affirmed were certain truths about humanity's ability to reason, and from that reason comes a sense of deon, or duty.

Immanuel Kant

Born in 1724 in Königsberg, Prussia (now part of Russia), Kant devoted almost his entire life to the pursuit of knowledge and deep understanding at the University of Königsberg, where he studied from age sixteen until just before his death in 1804. He also studied math and astronomy, but he was a pioneer in the philosophical subset of ethics, with books like *Critique of Pure Reason* (1781), *Critique of Practical Reason* (1788), and *Metaphysics of Morals* (1798).

SEPARATING ACTIONS
FROM OUTCOMES

One major way that deontology diverges from utilitarianism is that under utilitarianism, any action can be justified if it leads to happiness. (In other words, the ends justify the means.) Deontology presents a far more absolute view, in that some things, whatever they may be, are always wrong, and that even if an okay consequence results, it doesn't change the immoral nature of the action itself. As such, actions in deontology must always be judged independently from their outcomes.

Here's an example: A man walks by a yard and sees a dog that's been tied up and neglected. He decides to steal the dog, take it home, feed it, and treat it well. A utilitarian philosopher would argue that the man's theft was morally good, because the outcome was favorable—the dog (and probably the man) received happiness. But a Kantian or deontologist would argue that stealing is wrong, period. The outcome itself was a good one, but the nature of that outcome has little to nothing to do with the action that caused it—because it is objectively wrong to steal.

Quotable Voices

"Enlightenment is man's release from his self-incurred tutelage. Tutelage is man's inability to make use of his understanding without direction from another. Self-incurred is this tutelage when its cause lies not in lack of reason but in lack of resolution and courage to use it without direction from another. Sapere aude! 'Have courage to use your own reason!'—that is the motto of enlightenment."
—Immanuel Kant, on the path to enlightenment

Flip the situation around, and there's still a disconnect. Someone intending to do something objectively bad can accidentally create a good consequence. Let's change up the previous example. A man decides to steal a dog, and this he does, but he has no idea that the dog he stole was being mistreated by its previous owner. This objectively wrong act of theft saves the dog from mistreatment, and the result is a "good" outcome from a "bad" action.

GOODWILL TOWARD MEN

It's all well and good to separate an action from its outcome. But how is an action determined to be unambiguously morally right or wrong in the secular realm, without religious maxims to point the way? The seed of Kantianism is the idea that human beings alone have the capacity for reason. We can think things through and act based on our thoughts, and this ability empowers us with a sense of duty or moral obligation. These abilities supersede and diminish our animal instincts, which don't play a role in decision-making. Duty and obligation are so universal that they provide all of us with more or less the same system of rules that guide our actions and make us do the right thing, regardless of instinct, desire, or personal intentions. We intend to do good, or at least we have the will to do so. In other words, good intentions matter, and we are guided not by religious faith but by duty to our fellow man. Goodwill comes when a person commits an action out of "respect for the moral law," or in other words, one's duty.

To Kant, will is truly the only thing that is intrinsically good, or "good without qualification." The moral status of concepts that most people (and other schools of philosophy) would assume are quite good have a bit murkier status in Kantian philosophy. Intelligence and even pleasure are not intrinsically good, nor are they good without "qualification." Pleasure is suspect because there are so many kinds of pleasure, such as *schadenfreude*, the German term for deriving pleasure out of the suffering of others.

KANT AND THE CATEGORICAL IMPERATIVE

Being Ethical, One Step at a Time

Part of the basis of Kant's theories is that morality, or the idea of morality, is a natural outgrowth of rational thinking. In Kantian ethics, this is referred to as the Categorical Imperative. According to Kant, this sense of morality is the ultimate goal or objective by which people should live their lives. This Categorical Imperative is necessary for a rational being, and it is an unconditional "prime directive" to be followed, a thesis statement for life, and which should be followed without natural, animalistic desires or instincts getting in the way. Put another way, this thesis of life is a moral compass, or a way by which a human being understands what is morally right, and so behaves accordingly, despite that human nature allows us to do bad things (or at least heartless, animal-like things).

Consequently, because moral acts are rational, this means that immoral acts are thereby irrational. It doesn't mean that humans don't commit immoral acts, because obviously that happens. Rather, it means that immoral acts violate the Categorical Imperative and thus don't make a lot of sense.

Kant set forth the idea of how to determine and define the Categorical Imperative, or rather how to work toward it, or state what it is. Certain criteria must be met, such as that the motivation behind a moral choice must necessarily lead to action. What follows is a step-by-step procedure for determining if an action is a Categorical Imperative, set in the context of Kant's two primary methodologies for deciding if an act is ethical: the Formula of the Universal Law of Nature, and the Humanity Formula.

THE FORMULA OF THE UNIVERSAL LAW OF NATURE

The core of Kant's Formula of the Universal Law of Nature, when translated into English from the original German, says that we should "act as if the maxim of your actions were to become, through your will, a universal [law of nature]." Unpacked from academic-speak, Kant is saying that a Categorical Imperative determined through this method is any behavioral standard you expect from others that is something you must do too—no exceptions. For example, if you consider it morally wrong to eat meat, then by the Formula of the Universal Law of Nature, you would also find it immoral to eat meat yourself. (And then you would follow through on the Categorical Imperative and adopt a vegetarian lifestyle.) Kant suggests that a good law to follow yourself is one that could be universally acceptable, or, as he put it, an ascribed law of nature.

Another example, on the negative side: If you think it's okay to cheat in sports, then you'd have to be willing to accept—and expect—that everyone else was cheating too. As you go, so goes the rest of the world. But a worldview predicated on cheating would generate chaos and anarchy, and also, nobody likes cheating. For these reasons, cheating would not actually be an acceptable Categorical Imperative.

A STEP-BY-STEP PROCEDURE

Determining a Categorical Imperative in this way involves a step-by-step method. You must:

- Take an action. (For example, stealing a loaf of bread.)
- Determine the maxim or principle behind the action. (You are hungry.)
- Ask what would happen if that action was a universal rule. (Everyone can steal without consequence if and because they are hungry.)

Thus:

- If the universal application is reasonable, it's a moral action. If it's unreasonable, the action was immoral, and therefore not a Categorical Imperative.

Kant broke this idea down with four examples that represent a majority of the different kinds of human moral duties. They are:

- You borrow money from a friend and promise to return it later but fully intend to never pay it back. Using the previous steps, it quickly becomes clear that the action is made with selfishness and deceit in mind, and you would not find that to be universally acceptable behavior.
- You are driven to suicide by a difficult series of events in your life. You are, in effect, willfully shortening your life because to continue would bring more pain than pleasure. The motivation behind the act of self-destruction as Kant describes it, is one of

acting out of self-love. Kant says suicide does not fit the designation of law of nature, because self-love naturally leads to the preservation of life, not its destruction.

- You have natural talents but decide to live a life of sloth and laziness instead. This is quite simple—while everyone certainly could pursue (or not pursue!) a life of idleness, the structure of the world would fall apart and not persist, so it is not natural or moral to do this.

- In his fourth example, Kant identifies giving to the less fortunate as an actual, full-fledged example of something that qualifies as moral. The underlying principle is "I will help someone." Most people would be fine with this being a universally accepted example of something that's good. (It also takes into account each person's need, and even obligation, to receive help if they are the one in need.)

THE HUMANITY FORMULA

Kant's other main formulation for the Categorical Imperative is called the Humanity Formula. The explanation translates as: "Act in such a way that you always treat humanity, whether in your own person or in the person of any other, never simply as a mean, but always at the same time as an end." In other words, Kant suggests that humans ought to treat other human beings tenderly, carefully, and with great dignity—rather than as objects or as faceless, abstract examples of "humanity."

Some things have instrumental value, and others have inherent value. Instrumental value is a means to an end—a plastic spoon has little value in and of itself, but it has instrumental value in that it helps you place nourishing food into your mouth. Similarly, Kant says it's wrong to use other human beings to pursue our own needs because they're, well, human beings, and they have innate value apart from their interactions with others. This is due in large part because a person's innate value stems from his ability to set aside his animal instincts, and to thoughtfully shape his life and the lives of others. In other words, we have reason, and that gives us moral responsibility and innate value. Moral acts are ones that don't diminish the humanity of others, but instead actively help to increase that humanity.

David Hume (1711–1776)

Kant was greatly influenced by the works of Scottish philosopher David Hume. Kant is said to have conceived of his critical philosophy in direct reaction to Hume, stating that Hume had awakened him from his "dogmatic slumber." Hume thought that humans were creatures more of emotions and sentiment than creatures of reason.

The same examples used in the Formula of the Universal Law of Nature can also be used to suggest what acts are moral or immoral. Borrowing money with no intention of returning it makes an object out of another person, because doing so is exploitive and denies recognition of that person's inner value. Suicide and being lazy are selfish acts as well, as they rob a person of dignity—and that person might just happen to be you. Finally, failing to help others in need is dignity robbing, albeit by omission: you are not seeing them as a person and are ignoring their needs and, further, are not adding to or even maintaining their dignity.

ALTERNATE FORMULATIONS OF KANT'S CATEGORICAL IMPERATIVE

More Ways to Get Ethical

Because life is a complex web of situations, each with their own moral pros and cons that have to be figured out on a case-by-case basis, Kant, one of the most dominant thinkers of all time on the subject of ethics, didn't come up with a mere two ways to formulate a Categorical Imperative, the method by which one can decide whether or not an action is ethical. He devised four methodologies. The two previously discussed, the Formula of the Universal Law of Nature and the Humanity Formula, are generally very good methods. But life is complicated, and Kant came up with two more, although they are lesser used and are derivatives of the other two formulas. Hence, they are considered alternate formulations in the world of ethics.

AUTONOMY FORMULA

The first of these alternative, derivative formulations is the Formula of Autonomy. Translated from Kant's German, the crux is, "So act that your will can regard itself at the same time as making universal law through its maxims." Because this imperative brings up the concept and application of universal law right there in its explanation, this one is a derivative of a major point of the Formula of the Universal Law of Nature. But it also involves bits of the Humanity Formula as well, because it examines and defines what it means to be human: the gift and burden of rationality. With this formula, Kant really stresses his notion that human will rationally shapes the world. He suggests that an action can be determined to be moral if the action is worthy of the lofty status of human-as-rational-crafter-of-life-and-the-world. Kant says that humans are obligated to adhere to universal law because of (or in spite of) their free will to do so. This formula is all about our will to act, and to act apart from animal instinct or selfish needs—free will is rational, and that is what makes humans the most evolved and sophisticated animal.

Quotable Voices

"In law a man is guilty when he violates the rights of others. In ethics he is guilty if he only thinks of doing so." —Immanuel Kant

One of the arguments behind the Autonomy Formula is that a rational human would make himself adhere to good actions of his free will (or autonomy), freeing him from any other earthly desires or wants or religious dogma—because moral actions transcend this. Deciding if an action is moral is both up to the individual and not. Universal law, however, deals with the innate goodness of something, if applied. The Autonomy Formula introduces rational human will—if it's the will of a rational being, then the action is, by definition, moral. (Because human will is both good and rational.) The Autonomy Formula involves conforming to a natural, universal law, however that's defined.

KINGDOM OF ENDS FORMULA

The fourth and final formulation for the Categorical Imperative is called the Kingdom of Ends Formula. Kant states: "So act as if you were through your maxims a law-making member of a kingdom of ends." Kant, in effect, puts the power of deciding the universal laws into the hands of the individual, for all human beings are capable of that. Such is the universality of free will and rational thought, particularly involving previous Categorical Imperative definitions in how they apply to one person, so too do they apply to all of humanity.

Moreover, the point is that the morality of all binds people together, thereby making everyone a king of morality and influencer of thoughts and actions. As such, an action should be undertaken only if it adds to or contributes to a moral community. Intent matters too: Does the intent behind the action have moral weight? Could that intent, not necessarily the action, function as a universal law in the community—in this case the moral community of humanity? Kant again elevates humans, as our ability to reason out morality is what makes us the kings of the world. He defines animals as living in "realms of nature" while humans live in "realms of grace."

Thomas Hobbes (1588–1679)

Renowed English philosopher Thomas Hobbes is most famous for his ideas on social contract theory. In his most famous work *Leviathan,* Hobbes imagines what life would be like without a form of government, where each person would have the right to do anything in the world they wanted. Hobbes argues that such a state would lead to a "war of all against all." If people were only concerned with their own benefit, society would fall apart, people would be in constant fear of violent death, and humanity would become nasty and brutish. This is why, Hobbes argues, we need civil society.

Kant's connecting a moral code to rationality is nothing new—major philosophers such as Thomas Hobbes and Thomas Aquinas both previously linked them too. The difference is that Hobbes argued that morality was a way to help people achieve their desires, and Aquinas believed that rational, moral ideals were the result of the act of reasoning—an action, not so much something inherent. This is where Kant is different. He would argue that adhering to the Categorical Imperative, and a moral system, is vital to the entire process of acting like a rational human being. In fact, this adherence makes us human, for it shows we are much more sophisticated than animals, which cave to their immediate desires.

JOHN RAWLS AND THE ETHICS OF EGALITARIANISM

Justice and Fairness

Twentieth-century American philosopher John Rawls (1921–2002) advocated for a justice-centered moral philosophy. He argued that much of Western civilization's institutions and laws are based on some unassailable and universally agreed upon concept of "justice." Rawls called this the Original Position. He argued that this Original Position is a starting point for humans who wish to establish a society, or at least the rules to create a social order of that prospective culture. He contended that a group of humans set with the task to create some kind of social order would do so from a standpoint in which justice was paramount. That drive would lead to rules and institutions that would ensure the well-being of those they govern, not to mention, and this is important, their own well-being. In other words, Rawls took a cue from the Declaration of Independence: that all people are created equal. This is a moral philosophical concept—that manifests in the form of rules, à la Kant—called egalitarianism. Equality, ideally, then leads to justice.

THE LIBERTY PRINCIPLE

While a strict reading of egalitarianism would mean equal rights, justice, and treatment for all humans, no matter what, Rawls acknowledged that such a dream world is nice, but that it is not likely to happen. He knew that inequalities happen, but that they could at least be minimized by two principles, both outgrowths of the Original Position.

The first principle is the Liberty Principle. Rawls stated that the individual should have the right, in theory, to as many liberties as possible within the greater scope of a system that has a stated purpose of liberty for all. In other words, the individual has rights to live his life inasmuch as it doesn't infringe on the rights of others to live their lives and to seek their opportunities in much the same fashion.

THE DIFFERENCE PRINCIPLE

Rawls's other main principle derived from the Original Position is called the Difference Principle. Again, recognizing that inequalities and differences in wealth and standing are going to happen, Rawls found these disparities to be just fine, so long as those with more fulfill their due moral diligence, or obligation, to make up for those differences and even out things, if only a little, by helping those who do not have the advantages that they have had. Acting on the Difference Principle is what Rawls called "natural duties." Among these moral actions by which people must live their lives to maintain the moral equilibrium are not actively harming others, keeping promises, and helping those less fortunate than themselves. These ideals engender mutual respect and lead to an individual sense of justice in day-to-day life, as well as more formal political and legal systems to ensure that the basic needs of all humans are met.

Rawls's theories are an application of Kant's Kingdom of Ends approach. This is particularly true in Rawls's concept of justice as a form of fairness. As such, his theories are far more practical. Indeed, they are written with an eye toward adoption in the real-life political sphere. In this manner, Rawls is more of a political scientist than moral philosopher, although there could and should be overlap in the two disciplines if we want to create a fair and just society. (At least, there would be if Rawls had his way.)

Quotable Voices

"Each person possesses an inviolability founded on justice that even the welfare of society as a whole cannot override. For this reason, justice denies that the loss of freedom for some is made right by a greater good shared by others. It does not allow that the sacrifices imposed on a few are outweighed by the larger sum of advantages enjoyed by many." —John Rawls

THE VEIL OF IGNORANCE

Rawls is not the first philosopher or thinker to explore the idea of a social contract. As is the case with the larger discipline of ethics, social contract theorists generally come from a naturalistic viewpoint. That is, they look at how humanity would behave if it returned to a natural, and thereby idealistic, state. Rawls saw it a different way, rejecting the "state of nature" for an idea. He instead used a thought experiment to demonstrate his concepts, which he called the "Veil of Ignorance."

Rawls described this veil as a hypothetical state in which every individual has no idea (or is veiled in ignorance) of the benefits and weaknesses they would have in a society. They don't know about their own talents, their own disadvantages, their financial state, or even their race, gender, or religion. In other words, all biases have been eliminated. Rawls then asks us to consider how we would enjoy, or fit in, to such a society in which we have no prior knowledge of our own standing. The philosopher himself argued that we'd end up with a society where the disadvantaged would get extra help. Rawls attests that the less fortunate would be given the same rights as all, and that the only limitation would occur when property rights were threatened.

This leads into Rawls's Principle of Equality of Opportunity. He advocated that it is of ethical importance to provide for those who are least advantaged—especially due to biases regarding race, poverty, disabilities, and other inequalities—in our real-world societies. Such provisions include intervention at the government level, so as to ensure that decisions and policies are made with an openness to people from all walks of life.

CRITICISMS OF KANTIAN ETHICS

Those Who Can't Kant

Even Kant's detractors will admit that he was a brilliant philosopher who provided keen insights into how and why humans act, and how morality is not necessarily human nature, but that it is human nature to act morally because of the tools of free will and rationality. His determination and definitions of moral acts, by running them through one of four Categorical Imperative formulations, however clean, easy, and astute, had its share of critics who found some flaws. And these flaws have only served to extend the philosophical debate and cloud the idea of "morality" even further.

SCHOPENHAUER'S CONCERNS

Major nineteenth-century German philosopher Arthur Schopenhauer (1788–1860) agreed with many of Kant's positions on ethics, but not how he arrived at some of his conclusions. Schopenhauer found fault with the Categorical Imperative. Despite four very intricately detailed methodologies for determining how and why an act was moral or not, not to mention the reasoning behind even the decision that led to the decision about whether an act was moral, Schopenhauer argued that Kant's argument with the Categorical Imperative boiled down to (or reduced to, in philosophical parlance), "Don't do stuff to other people if you wouldn't be okay with it being done to you." In other words, the Categorical Imperative, to Schopenhauer, was the Golden Rule, reworded in intellectual trappings.

One of Schopenhauer's main arguments was that human actions aren't always guided by the same thing—that sometimes humans are driven by selfishness, but just as often by sympathy or empathy. Schopenhauer found there to be a great deal of sympathy in unimpeachably moral actions, and that it was just as humanizing a thing as Kant's free will. Kant didn't write much about sympathy, agreeing with Schopenhauer that it is an emotion, and that there's little place for the hard-to-quantify things like emotions in an objective argument about what is or isn't moral. In other words, feelings are unstable and unreliable, and thus can't provide a bedrock for a moral code. But Schopenhauer argued that denying feelings like sympathy leads to an increased egoism, which clouds judgment. He suggested that sympathy is necessary in determining how to act in a moral way toward one's fellow man.

Arthur Schopenhauer (1788–1860)

Schopenhauer was among the most notable European philosophers of the nineteenth century. His masterwork was *The World as Will and Representation*, and it laid out one of the author's most innovative contributions to philosophy. Namely, that human action is driven, and not always to happiness or success, by a restless, unhappy individual will.

HEGEL'S ISSUES

Georg Wilhelm Friedrich Hegel (1770–1831) was, almost immediately out of the gate, a critic of Kant's universal theories. Like Schopenhauer, Hegel had some problems with the Formula of the

Universal Law of Nature. He was uncomfortable with how Kant, in his attempt to humanize morality, dehumanized morality. He said the formula consists of "empty formalism" and that "moral science is converted into mere rhetoric about duty for duty's sake." In other words, it spoke too much of moral actions in the abstract without really defining what a moral action is, leaving it entirely up to the interpretation of the reader. For Hegel, the Categorical Imperative is too much of a morality test, and it lacks a contradiction for the sake of argument. It's too bland and idealistic for Hegel's tastes.

MILL'S CRITIQUES

A third major philosopher who had problems with the far too open-ended Categorical Imperative formulation was nineteenth-century British philosopher John Stuart Mill. While Kant's arguments were a contradictory argument to utilitarianism, Mill argued that with a little picking, Kant's Categorical Imperative formulations reduced to…utilitarianism. Kant believed that morality was a result of reasoning ability, and that the agent didn't need to take into consideration the effects of those actions on the perpetrator—in other words, the person who did the actions. Kant was all about the ability to reason and its effects on others, but did not concern himself much on the self, or our happiness.

Mill was a bit more realistic in considering a human's natural ability and need to focus on the self. He thought moral duties took their cues from a consideration of how they would affect happiness, both of others, as well as our own. This, of course, is a utilitarian principle: actions are morally right mostly in regard to how much happiness they promote toward the end goal of happiness.

FREUD ON KANT

Philosophers have long butted heads with scientists over the true nature of the world—one group tries to look within, or to the unseen, for answers about the universe around them, while the other gathers physical proof to make the same grand statements about the true nature of the world. These are two wildly disparate approaches, and one major scientific thinker had a big problem with some of Kant's arguments. Austrian neurologist Sigmund Freud (1856–1939) is widely regarded as the father of psychology, which is the study of the human mind. In many ways, psychology is a scientifically grounded form of ethics in that it also seeks to determine why humans might behave the way they do, albeit from a biological perspective.

While many of his theories are no longer taken as fact by the mainstream psychological community, Freud wrote extensively on the nature of the human unconscious and its role in determining behavior. Freud wrote that the human psyche, or our mental being, consists of three parts that were often in conflict: the id, the ego, and the superego. The id consists of basic instincts and pleasure-seeking behaviors; the ego seeks to please the id in culturally acceptable ways; the superego contains the internalization of cultural rules and the ways one ought to behave, or morals. Freud disagreed with Kant's idea that a moral sense of duty is innate. He held that those ideas came from the superego, which rewards good behavior. In this regard, being moral due to a sense of duty is a mental "neurosis" to please the psyche and not out of any kind of deeply held sense of duty or purpose.

Chapter 5

VIRTUE ETHICS

Theories that fall under the heading of virtue ethics are all an evolution and exploration of philosophical themes first outlined thousands of years ago in the writings of Aristotle. In virtue ethics, moral fortitude is based on rules, but only because the rules are applied by the agent, or person. Virtue ethics is agent based, because agents use a moral code they've adopted for themselves, and that moral code is made up of true, honorable, and just virtues that guide their actions. Most of these virtues are qualities (which are, by nature, positive or "quality" character traits) that the individual's culture or society has ingrained upon him or her as being very important. These virtues are the building blocks of a truly moral individual.

Understanding virtue ethics begins by recalling deontological theories. Like virtue ethics, deontological theories involve living by steadfastly held moral truths. In deontology, these virtues are examined closely so as to become second nature, and used to develop good, moral character habits. In virtue ethics, by contrast, those ethics don't require thought or careful planning or thinking because they become second nature and affect, in theory, every thought and action an individual undertakes without the individual even realizing it.

Although it's difficult to find universal truths about most any aspect of ethics, the same cannot be said for virtues. How virtues are applied and defined may vary wildly from person to person, culture to culture, or era to era, but certain character traits nonetheless have become bona fide virtues due to their almost universal acceptance and admiration. Such character traits that are turned into virtues include things like wisdom, generosity, justice, temperance, keeping a level head, and kindness. Another virtue that's important in applied ethics is passing on those virtues: it's virtuous for adults to pass on virtues to their children, as it is their responsibility to do so.

Some of the ethical notions that come under the "virtue ethics" umbrella that we'll discuss in this chapter include:

- **Divine command theory,** the idea that all good behaviors—and the virtues that guide them—are laid out explicitly by a divine figure, such as God. If God said it's good, it's good, and if God said it's bad, it's bad.
- **Natural law ethics,** a theory developed by Thomas Aquinas that finds human nature is one and the same with the ethical goodness, and that it is human nature to adopt virtues and act virtuously.
- **Relativism,** the notion that virtues—and thus ethical strictures—can vary from culture to culture because of the different values and needs of each culture. Relativism holds that it's not correct to judge or make statements about absolutes.
- **Moral realism** is an opposing viewpoint to relativism. Under this philosophy, there are some moral truths and values that are objectively good, whether or not an individual or even community chooses to accept them as such. (Moral antirealism then is the idea that there are no objectively morally right virtues.)

VIRTUE ETHICS

It's Good to Be Good

So far we've covered two of the three primary approaches to moral philosophy, or ethics. More specifically, we've discussed mainstream or normative ethics. We have also examined deontological ethics and utilitarian ethics. This leaves us, finally, with virtue ethics, which is also called virtue theory.

Let us return for a moment to a few of the ethics theories we've discussed. Recall that deontology seeks to find the secrets of ethics with rules and duties, and consequentialism and utilitarianism are about the potential ramifications (good or bad) of human actions. A utilitarian would point to a person needing help and find that the consequences of helping maximizes well-being, suggesting a positive moral act. A deontologist will help a person if doing so follows the moral rule that it is good and right to help. Deontology provides a subtle but important difference from virtue ethics.

A virtue ethicist acts because helping another is charitable, benevolent, or just the "right" thing to do. It's a virtue-based, not rule-based ethic. The ideas or principles behind the rules that a deontologist sets are what a virtue ethicist follows, and similarly, such rules are what must be followed. Or perhaps it's the other way around? That is: the deontologists make and follow their rules based on the virtues that the virtue ethicists established. All three approaches to ethics make room for virtues, especially deontology, because virtues inform those rules that must be adhered to. (Any good normative ethical theory will have something to say about all three concepts.) What makes virtue ethics different, and its own discipline, is the centrality of virtue in the theory itself. The others use virtues as a means to an end, not the end in and of itself.

THE NEED FOR VIRTUES

Virtue ethics were the dominant school in moral philosophy until the Enlightenment of Europe in the eighteenth century, and, after falling out favor somewhat, they returned to become the dominant school in the twenty-first century. Perhaps this is because the moral philosophy of virtue ethics is the only major school that takes into consideration the interplays between virtues and vices, motives and morality, moral education, wisdom and discernment, relationships, a concept of happiness, and what sorts of persons we ought to be.

Defined simply, a virtue is a highly regarded personality trait or aspect of character. While many so-called virtues are almost universal, they are broadly defined as a deeply held value by a person that intrinsically leads him or her to behave in a certain way. Virtues affect how we absorb the world around us and act in the world. Virtues influence actions, feelings, desires, choices, and reactions—all of which are predictable in a person, if that value is deeply held. And while these values may lead a person to act out instinctively, they are learned behaviors that are well thought out and deeply felt on the level of a religious belief. The most precious virtues seem like they are intrinsic to a person's nature, so affirmed they can be. These virtues are authentic and adhere to rules that are nice for the way people live and function together in a society. These virtues also take feelings into consideration, as well as personal well-being and the well-being of others. (Contrast this approach to deontology with its assertion that "the rule says it's right.")

Virtuous people are not perfect, but this does not affect the purity or inspirational component of the virtue itself. In its application, human frailty, weaknesses, and contradictions come into play. This is due to the very human lack of practical wisdom or moral wisdom. Such knowledge could also be called applied wisdom, as these actions demonstrate virtues. Virtuous actions make a person good, and it is those actions that make a person good, not just good intentions, as other ethical schools may argue.

The Ten Essential Virtues

The ancient Greeks named ten virtues to be the most essential. They are: wisdom, justice, fortitude, self-control, love, positivity, hard work, integrity, gratitude, and humility.

There are a few different approaches to virtue ethics, although each shares the same core argument in putting virtues first and foremost. The three approaches that concern us here are eudaimonism, ethics of care, and agent-based theories.

EUDAIMONISM

In ancient Greece, and up through the medieval era, the type of virtue ethics now called eudaimonism was synonymous with virtue ethics. This approach holds that the ideal goal of human existence is individual *eudaimonia*, which translates variously (but similarly) to "happiness" or "well-being" or "the good life." This goodness is attainable by the acting out of those virtues (which the Greeks called *phronesis*) day in and day out in one's thoughts and actions. The main problem is that eudaimonia, or happiness, is vaguely defined, self-defined, and quite subjective. It's hard to have a universal approach to the ethical outlook of humanity if everyone defines the goal differently. What is objective and seemingly universal, however, is that phronesis is the tool by which happiness can be achieved. However, good intentions are not enough—one must act ethically to be ethical.

ETHICS OF CARE

Another form of virtue ethics is ethics of care. It's a relatively recent addition to the world of ethics, and it was developed in the late twentieth century as an outgrowth of feminist theory, particularly the works of Annette Baier (1929–2012). The theory supposes that normative gender roles influence the way a person thinks and acts, particularly as it concerns that person's ethical outlook. Generally speaking, men form philosophies based on linear, "masculine" ideals such as justice and personal autonomy, which are more abstract, objective, and less emotionally based or sympathetic. Women, on the other hand, may think less linearly, and consider whole beings and take empathy and care into consideration more so than masculine-based ideals. Ethics of care argues for an approach to moral philosophy from a more traditionally "female" viewpoint—and that the most important virtues are taking care of others, being patient and nurturing, and being willing to sacrifice one's own happiness so as to bring happiness to others. Out go universal standards established over the course of thousands of years by a male-thought dominated society, and in come the virtuous ideas of community and relationship-building from a female point of view. In such a female viewpoint, the interests of those close to us take on importance with our own interests, although they are still above those of strangers (although the community can and should always be growing so as to become ever more unified).

AGENT-BASED THEORIES

The third type of virtue ethics fall under the umbrella of agent-based theories. A twentieth-century development, primarily by philosopher Michael Slote, these theories rely on creating virtues from commonsense notions about what virtues are. This approach uses the largest, the most normal, and the most lauded virtues across time and culture. Such general virtues, for example, include being kind and showing mercy. Agent-based theories move the burden of ethics to the inner life of the agents who perform those actions, and away from the interpreter of the moral philosophy. Virtue-based ethics exist in other, morally decent people, and so we try to be more like them, as we do our best to embody and adopt their virtues as our own.

CRITICISMS OF VIRTUE ETHICS

Virtues Without Virtues

Virtue ethics is the oldest, arguably most basic of all moral philosophy theories, with other methods and schools branching off from it to address the increasingly sophisticated world and increasingly sophisticated demands of human nature. Not only have concepts like deontology sprouted up to address the perceived flaws of virtue ethics, but some writers and philosophers have some issues with the structure of virtue ethics itself. (Very few have a problem with virtues.) Generally speaking, virtues are, by definition, "good" universal values that all of us should try to have, or already have; academically speaking, virtues are just a little too open-ended and difficult to interpret for some.

THE SUBJECT OF SUBJECTIVITY

One major problem with virtue ethics is the subjective, relative nature of individual virtues. Across cultures, races, time, and other major factors, it's hard to find virtues, let alone any single virtue, that absolutely everyone can agree on. Critics of virtue ethics could convincingly argue that it's simply not possible to have a universally accepted list of virtues. It's difficult to separate virtues from the circumstances that created them, which in turn makes it difficult to make them apply equally across time, space, and culture. For example, being a good warrior is a virtue in ancient Greece, but in a present-day pacifist society...not so much.

A LACK OF ACTION

Another criticism of virtue ethics is that it's not action-oriented, or even action-suggesting. It's too focused on the ideas behind actions without providing much guidance into how those virtues should play out. Virtue ethics, it is argued, almost trusts that virtuous people will simply act in a virtuous way because they are virtuous. This makes virtue ethics not as good an ethical foundation for creating laws as, say, deontology, because in deontology virtues evolved into rules with reasoning behind them. In virtue ethics, its critics note, virtues represent little more than "nice" ways that people "should" act, but without a lot of argument as to why, or even consequences if they don't.

INDIVIDUAL ISSUES

Is virtue ethics too heavily based on the individual rather than on society at large? That's a potentially problematic situation for a method that purports to determine universal ethical truths. Virtue ethics is all about an individual's personal strength of character. The effect that a person's actions, even virtue-led actions, have on the world around him or her does not much factor into virtue ethics. It is a self-centered method, critics allege, because it's about the benefit to the self, not others. (The exception would be ethics of care, which represents a reasonable solution to this dilemma.)

One other major problem in virtue ethics is that it presents the world as a collection of positive hypotheticals, and that in turn supposes that everyone has control of their own fate and destiny, and that, if their actions are good, good actions will come. Virtue ethics says nothing of how others' actions affect an individual, not to mention how luck or the often random nature of the universe affects a person. Because of the complex nature of the world and because life is sometimes unfair and unlucky, good things just kind of happen to bad people sometimes, just as bad things happen to good people. Of course, some people aren't raised with a support system, for example, and so they don't get the help they need to foster their humanity or moral maturity. This is no fault of their own. Virtue ethics doesn't much address these issues, although it does contain an element of moral luck, arguing that virtues are in fact vulnerable, if not fragile.

Quotable Voices

"[V]irtues are not simply dispositions to behave in specified ways, for which rules and principles can always be cited. In addition, they involve skills of perception and articulation, situation-specific 'know-how,' all of which are developed only through recognizing and acting on what is relevant in concrete moral contexts as they arise….Due to the very nature of the moral virtues, there is thus a very limited amount of advice on moral quandaries that one can reasonably expect from the virtue-oriented approach." —Robert Louden, "Some Vices of Virtue Ethics"

OTHER ISSUES

Apart from all these theoretical issues surrounding virtue ethics is a very real-world problem with their application. Virtues don't exist in a vacuum, and rarely is one virtue the only one employed to solve an ethical issue or in making a decision. And it's a very real possibility, if not a probability, that two or more virtues will clash. This is problematic, as virtues are mostly of equal merit. For example, honesty is a virtue, but then so is compassion. But what if you're required to tell the truth, even if it's going to hurt somebody's feelings? You either tell the truth and feelings are hurt, or you lie to spare someone's hurt feelings. Whatever situational choice you make, you've chosen one virtue over the other. As this example illustrates, this is one area in which virtue ethics can fail.

DIVINE COMMAND THEORY

As It Is Written

One of the things that makes moral philosophy or ethics such a unique subset of philosophy is its focus on the individual's application of the truth, and his or her role in spreading the truth. Other parts of philosophy are all about truth and purpose as abstract concepts; it's ethics where those ideals play out in real-world thoughts and actions. Ethics asks, "How do we, as humans, utilize this truth in how we behave?"

There happens to be one ethical school that makes figuring all that out just a little bit easier. In divine command theory, people are supposed to do what God says is right, and should not do what God says is wrong. It's as simple as that. Of course, doing that day in and day out isn't simple, as any deeply religious person can tell you.

Divine command theory states that the ethical thing to do is what a divine figure would do, or has told you to do. A lot of it has been laid out in the form of holy texts, but not everything is there, and especially not for modern problems in a changing world. That's why, in terms of discussion and debate, divine command theory is just as complicated and profound as the other schools of ethics.

WORD FROM ON HIGH

Many schools of ethics factor in several different criteria when considering whether or not an act is moral. They use a sliding scale that involves things like happiness, law of the land, objective morality of an act, and limiting damage. Divine command theory, by contrast, rejects all that stuff because it's simply not as important as the word of God. In divine command theory, an act is considered moral or immoral based solely on God's judgment about it. For example, if God says stealing is wrong, then stealing is wrong. Moreover, no ethical debates enter into the arena to address gray areas, even ones where morality comes into play. Take, for example, stealing again. Since all stealing is wrong in this hypothetical scenario, then it would be wrong to steal, period, even to feed a starving child.

Augustine and Divine Command Theory

Augustine (354–430) was a philosopher and theologian early in the development of the Christian Church. He combined early Christian teachings with some elements of Neoplatonism and laid down the basics for divine command theory as a philosophical framework, providing specifics and rationale beyond the overly simplistic idea of "because God said so." To Augustine (later St. Augustine, per the Roman Catholic Church), ethics could be defined as the quest for "supreme" goodness, which in turn provides the happiness that humans are forever seeking out.

DIVINITY VERSUS RELIGION

While it is somewhat refreshing to find a moral theory that has definite absolutes and doesn't get hung up on middle ground (the importance of intent or semantics, to name some philosophical issues), divine command theory is not a very workable theory because it is so incredibly black and white. It is the essence of idealism to view, approach, and act so bilaterally in a world almost universally acknowledged—even by those who believe in a powerful divine entity—to be complex and complicated.

Divine command theory is not religion, or at least not exactly. It's a principle of religion. Modern, organized religions certainly have an element of divine command theory in their dogma, but they provide nuanced systems of life rules, cultural and social histories, and theology, as well as moral philosophy. Very few religions in the twenty-first century take a "yes/no" approach to moral and ethical actions. This is the result of centuries of debate about the nature of the world and the godhead of each religion, which is believed to have had a hand in its creation. Religious thought in circles that have remained relevant are the ones that have kept pace with philosophy in recognizing that there is very little black and white in the world. Take killing, for example. Murder is recognized as bad in Christianity, but ministers and priests are embedded with troops in times of war to provide comfort and guidance to those whose job it is to kill. There are layers to everything, and divine command theory doesn't always allow for the recognition of that.

THE EUTHYPHRO DILEMMA

The Euthyphro dilemma is a classic ethical exercise that demonstrates the flaws of divine command theory (but not the religions upon which it is based). Outlined in a dialogue with an Athenian man named Euthyphro by the ancient Greek philosopher Plato, this dilemma centers on the ethical question of intent versus the absolute purity of an act. For example, is murder wrong because, as divine command theory would argue, God has banned it? Or is it the other way around—does God prohibit murder because it is intrinsically wrong to take the life of another? In the Euthyphro dilemma, Plato argues the latter: that a just and moral God would go ahead and prohibit an act that is wrong because it's innately wrong, and would not make such declaration as a mere exercise for stretching divine muscles.

However, this throws a wrench into divine command theory, or at least its need to exist. If certain acts are moral or immoral regardless of whether or not God deems them so, then God is not necessary. Those acts are moral or immoral and have nothing at all to do with God, who divinely orders (or forbids) them. In short, divine command theory does not do what moral philosophy sets out to do—determine which morals are objectively true—but instead undermines the ethical motivation by saying that actions don't require any justification beyond "God said so."

IT'S ALL SUBJECTIVE

Oddly, divine command theory is a type of moral relativism. This is because it ties morality to a particular religion's figurehead, while also making ethical decisions subjective. As in moral relativism, what is right for one culture may not be right for another. That holds true in divine command theory, because what is right or what is wrong is up to God, a completely external force in the world. It also exposes ethics for what they may truly be: opinions. If God stated that a known fact was wrong, such as $2 + 2 = 4$, then under the tenets of divine command theory that statement would be true, even though it's objectively and empirically false. In other words, in this moral philosophy there is no standard or judgment of something other than it being God's command.

THOMAS AQUINAS AND NATURAL LAW ETHICS

Doing What Comes Naturally

Natural law ethics is an approach to moral philosophy that takes its cues from the ways of nature and the natural world. Now, this does not mean that we should simply do "what comes naturally." That's a pretty tricky thing to define anyway—a lot of ethics and philosophy is concerned with trying to figure out just what "nature" or "human nature" is, and if that nature can be changed, developed, or forced to evolve. Rather, in the school of natural law moral theory, the idea is that the moral standards or expectations that govern human behavior ought to be objectively derived from the nature of human beings and the world. We act the way we do because, well, that's the way we act. Natural law theory adherents believe it's best to figure out what that means and apply it to everything from politics to the law to religious dogma. (Put another, more cynical way, this theory is as dismissive and dispassionate as chalking up bad behavior to the maxim that "boys will be boys.")

Quotable Voices

"We can't have full knowledge all at once. We must start by believing; then afterwards we may be led on to master the evidence for ourselves." —Thomas Aquinas

THE DIFFERENT TYPES OF LAWS

At the forefront of natural law theory are the writings of Thomas Aquinas (1225–1274). He attested that we are the way we are and act the way we act because God, or at least the Christian conception of God, is what made us that way.

In one of his major texts, *Summa Theologica*, Aquinas posits that there are four types of natural laws that govern the universe and everything in it. They are eternal law, natural law, human law, and divine law.

- **Eternal law** is what keeps the universe, or *kosmos* in Greek, in proper working order. It exists, as it always has, and always will, says Aquinas, within the mind of God (who Aquinas calls Logos).
- **Natural law** is the contribution and participation by the rational creature (man) in the eternal law. Aquinas argues that this ability to help the natural order of things hum along is imprinted on us as rational beings.
- **Human law** is different from natural law, which is essentially the essence of humanity. Human law, however, is the morally-based earthly laws by which human societies function.
- **Divine law** is how eternal law is applied, and Aquinas says that this is all the will of God, and it's laid out plainly in the Old Testament and New Testament.

THE IMPORTANCE OF DIVINITY

Aquinas's fourth law, divine law, offers a specific plan of action. Like the difference between normative ethics and descriptive ethics, the difference between eternal law and divine law is a matter of theory versus action. Aquinas argues that divine law (and Christianity, and the Bible) is crucial, because humans need divine guidance on how to act correctly because of another aspect of our nature, namely our innate uncertainty and incompetence. Aquinas also clearly lays out that old chestnut of ethical arguments: that there are consequences for our actions that we need to be made aware of.

On Thomas Aquinas (1225–1274)

Thomas Aquinas, or St. Thomas Aquinas, as he's known within the Catholic Church, was both a theologian as well as a philosopher. His writings uniquely combined the tenets of Christianity and faith with the notions of reason and rationality. As such, he's regarded as a pillar in a theological approach called Thomism as well as a pillar of the neoclassical, logic-based Aristotelian philosophical movement of Scholasticism, which combines both cultural religious tradition as well as church dogma.

Siddhartha Gautama, also known as Buddha, is the primary figure of Buddhism. Siddhartha sat under a Bodhi tree and vowed not to arise until he had found the truth. After forty-nine days he is said to have attained enlightenment. The teachings of this enlightened Buddha include the Four Noble Truths and the Noble Eightfold Path, and they form the basis of Buddhist ethics.

Top: Confucius, an influential Chinese philosopher, sought to reinforce the values of compassion and tradition based on the principle of *jen*, or loving others.

Photo Credit: © Getty Images/georgeclerk

Bottom: The term *ethics* comes from the Greek word *ethos*, meaning habit or custom. In fact, ancient Greece, and the city of Athens in particular, is thought to be the birthplace of Western philosophical ethics.

Photo Credit: © 123RF/sborisov

Top: Protagoras, depicted in this painting by Salvator Rosa, was one of the first Sophists (an ancient Greek teacher who used the tools of philosophy and rhetoric to teach). Protagoras is known for causing great controversy in ancient times through his statement "Man is the measure of all things." This phrase is often interpreted as meaning there is no absolute truth except what each individual person believes to be the truth.

Photo Credit: © Salvator Rosa [Public Domain] via Wikimedia Commons

Bottom: The *taijitu*, or yin/yang symbol, represents how the universe works. The universe is composed of a series of opposites, yins and yangs. These opposing forces are always in motion, swirling and moving into each other in this fluid and interconnected way. One opposite cannot exist without the other, nor is either one superior to the other. There is good and there is evil, there is pleasure and there is pain, and these things can only exist in relation to each other.

Photo Credit: © Getty Images/Nataiki

Thomas Aquinas is credited with trying to marry the ethical philosophies of the ancients, particularly Aristotle, with the teachings of the Catholic Church. As a result, he is credited with creating a moral philosophy for Christianity while contributing to the development of Western philosophy in general.

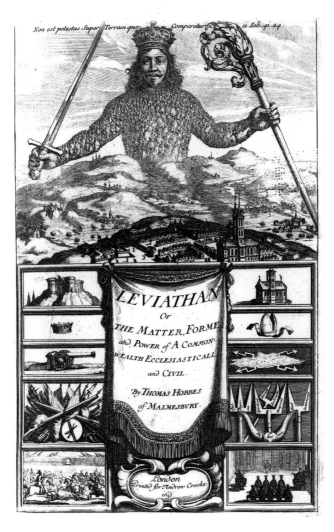

The book *Leviathan* is regarded as one of the earliest and most influential examples of social contract theory (the ethical and philosophical questioning of the legitimacy of the authority of the state over the individual). Written by English philosopher Thomas Hobbes in 1651, this work marks for many the beginning of modern political philosophy.

Voltaire was a French poet, novelist, and playwright who used his works to praise civil liberties and the separation of church and state. He supported civil liberties, most prominently freedom of religion and social reform. Voltaire leaned toward libertinism and hedonism—the philosophy that pleasure and the pursuit of pleasure is the point of life.

Photo Credit: © Nicolas de Largillière [Public Domain] via Wikimedia Commons

David Hume was a Scottish philosopher, historian, and essayist who believed that moral decisions are based on moral sentiment. In other words, feelings govern ethical actions, not reason.

Photo Credit: © Getty Images/denisk0

Top: Immanuel Kant was a German philosopher and a central figure in modern Western philosophy. Kant believed human understanding is the source of the general laws of nature that structure the human experience. Human reason therefore gives itself moral law, which is the basis of our belief in God, freedom, and immortality. Therefore science, morality, and religion are all mutually consistent because they all rest on the same foundation.

Bottom: Immanuel Kant was the first philosopher of note to teach at a university for the majority of his career. Kant taught at the University of Königsberg for over fifteen years. Though bigger universities tried to woo him away, he stayed at Königsberg, preferring to teach in his native land. The university was left in ruins after World War II and was rebuilt. Today it is known as Immanuel Kant Baltic Federal University.

Immanuel Kant

Top: Jean-Paul Sartre and his partner Simone de Beauvoir challenged the cultural and ethical assumptions of the post–World War II world. Sartre's primary idea was that people were "condemned to be free" and were "things in themselves," meaning that people receive no interference from a higher power, and that they are responsible for all of their actions, good or evil, without excuse.

Photo Credit: © Liu Dong'ao (Xinhua News Agency) [Public Domain] via Wikimedia Commons

Bottom: Sartre believed in socialist ideals and the labor party. He supported a number of leftist movements, one of which, in a move to protest the price hike at the Paris metro that directly impacted French workers, stole metro tickets and gave them away to workers. In memory of that act, visitors often leave their metro tickets on Sartre's grave in Paris out of reverence to his fight for the common man.

Photo Credit: © Liu Dong'ao (Xinhua News Agency) [Public Domain] via Wikimedia Commons

ETHICAL RELATIVISM

It's All Universally Specific

Ethical relativism is an interesting concept in moral philosophy because it is made up entirely of contradictions as well as comparisons. The theory acknowledges the universality of ethics, and the need for ethics in both the individuals and the societies in which they live—which is the problem. There are so many ethical constructs and maxims that it's difficult if not impossible to find universal ethical truths across the whole of human existence. Take killing, for example: some societies (or individuals) may find it to be reprehensible to take the life of another. Another society (or individual) can justify killing—such as in war, or if it were an accident. Another society, perhaps a warrior society from centuries ago, may think it's perfectly fine to take the life of another. Every action depends on its circumstances, moral philosophers would agree, and varying circumstances distinguish one culture from one another. This is ethical relativism—that there are no moral principles that are universally valid at all times to all people around the world and throughout all time.

WHERE APPROPRIATE

A culture, over time, develops its core values, virtues, and principles. And one culture develops independently of other cultures, and the values and virtues and principles of each culture are deemed to be generally acceptable, based on the needs of that particular society. Because of that, one cannot apply the ethical code (or what have you) from one society to another, because these codes are custom built, so to speak. Nor would one culture's set of codes make a lot of sense to another culture. The feudal code of Japan, for example, would not make much sense as an ethical code in present-day America. It's from a different culture, and a different time.

Quotable Voices

"The words 'vice' and 'virtue' supply us only with local meanings. There is no action, however bizarre you may picture it, that is truly criminal; or one that can really be called virtuous. Everything depends on our customs and on the climates we live in." —The Marquis de Sade, *The Immortal Mentors* (1796)

This means that the search for universal ethical truths is largely futile, and that the true work in developing ethics is to come up with ethical codes for the individual within a specific society, or for that specific society itself. Ethics cannot and should not be applied to other times, because it's all relative, and simply not fair to do so.

HERE COMES THE SCIENCE

Unlike many other moral philosophies, which, at the end of the day, are highly subjective, flawed, and even abstract, moral relativism has a certain amount of backup from science and history. An anthropologist could point to any number of behaviors that vary widely on the acceptability spectrum from one culture to another. Take polygamy for example. To have multiple wives is illegal in the present-day United States, reflecting the widespread ethical opinion that it's immoral to do so, for whatever reason that may be. Perhaps polygamy is forbidden because it is not a traditional lifestyle in the West; perhaps it is forbidden because certain religious groups in the 1800s that practiced it were considered to be outlandish for other reasons and this behavior was merely an example of that, and so polygamy was banned outright by the larger culture.

Moral relativism cautions us to remember context. Those religious groups in the 1800s may have found polygamy to be perfectly acceptable because without it they could not have perpetuated their society. As such, polygamy for them was a biological and dogmatic imperative. As uncomfortable as it may sound, the act of polygamy simply can't be deemed immoral just because whole communities have condoned or condemned it. As our anthropologist might remind us, we enter into a relatively gray ethical area when we deem something to be okay for one person or group, but not for others.

PROBLEMS WITH RELATIVISM

Despite the evidence to the contrary, such as the previous examples, by and large ethicists do not believe the idea of ethical relativism. This is because the academic pursuit of ethics is, by its nature, about finding universal truths of what it means to be human, however obscure. The rejection of ethical relativism also has something to do with the underlying moral principles behind the acts themselves. One example would be killing the elderly when they become infirm. While one society may find this literal action to be okay and another society may not, they both may agree on the reason for feeling the way they do. The elder-killing society does so due to an underlying principle—perhaps their religious beliefs say that the afterlife is more enjoyable if they enter while still somewhat physically active, or maybe they considered such killings to be a form of mercy that prevent the pains and indignities of advanced aging. In short, they care about the well-being of their elderly. The second society cares about their elderly too, and they show it by leaving them alone to die naturally, in their own time.

What's more, antirelativists can simply call out a society as doing something that is wrong and immoral. It doesn't matter if such society thinks the action is okay—some actions are fundamentally wrong, according to these critics. Take slavery for example. It is the overwhelming position of modern-day Americans that pre–Civil War era slavery was wrong, even though a lot of the country at the time believed it was okay. Slavery is wrong, and it doesn't matter if some people think it's okay today or thought it was okay at a given time in history. The point is that by declaring absolutes, we call into question the veracity of ethical relativism.

MORAL REALISM AND ANTIREALISM

Hard Truths and Constructs

Most topics that fall under the heading of moral philosophy or ethics concern applied ethics or normative ethics. Investigations into these topics seek to discover what specific actions and motivations are moral or are not moral. Metaethics is a branch of philosophy that looks at the creation of those morals. It concerns the nature, structure, history, and building blocks of morality.

GETTING MORALLY REAL

A dominant metaethical topic is moral realism, also called moral objectivism. Adherents argue that there is little relativism, individuality, or circumstance as far as ethics are concerned. Rather, they posit that there are steadfast moral truths and universal moral values—and that they are objectively good, regardless of an individual or community's shared acceptance or rejection of them.

A major advantage of moral realism is that it is almost mathematical or scientific in its approach. Because the idea of true versus not true, or fact or not fact, enters into it, logic can be applied to moral statements to see if they're truly moral or not. As such, there isn't room for more than one thing to be right, as is often the case with philosophy. It's a very linear, stringent outlook with not a lot of room to grow or stretch. (As such, some of the philosophers known for very strict or narrow worldviews could be considered moral realists, such as Immanuel Kant, Karl Marx, and Ayn Rand.)

There are obviously problems with this approach—while moral realism can settle an argument over the morality of an action (at least via its own internal logic), it does little to explain how the issue came about in the first place. Furthermore, moral facts aren't really facts, the way scientific, mathematic, or historical facts are facts, because they're unobservable. If a moral fact is unobservable, the scientific method can't truly be used to investigate, because observation is a crucial component of that method.

ETHICAL NATURALISM

Moral realism breaks down into two major variants. The first is ethical naturalism. This theory holds that clearly definable concepts are morally acceptable or unacceptable, and that is just part of their nature. These are cold, hard truths about morality, and they remain objectively true, whether individual people choose to follow them or not. They must be expressed as natural properties and without ethics terms and signifiers like "good" or "right." They just "are," no judgments imposed. Ethical naturalism supposes that certain ethical concepts are just a part of nature, and that observance of both humanity and the natural world will increase our knowledge of this. In this regard, ethics can be a kind of science.

Critics, being critics and all, have some problems with this assertion, particularly in terms of semantics. British philosopher G.E. Moore (1873–1958), for example, said that ethical terms are by their nature loaded words, and that, for example, something can't be defined as objectively good, because good is a "positive" word.

"Good" cannot be defined by unbiased words, like the descriptive words a geologist would use to describe, say, a rock or a mountain. This potential roadblock is called a "naturalistic fallacy"—and concepts like "good" must be left utterly indefinable.

ETHICAL NON-NATURALISM AND INTUITIONISM

In response to ethical naturalism, G.E. Moore helped craft an ethical doctrine called ethical non-naturalism. The crux of this doctrine is that ethical statements can only really express propositions that can't reduce to a nonethical statement. For example, "bad" can't really be defined or even quantified because it can't be defined by words other than synonyms for itself. However, ethical non-naturalism still relates to ethical naturalism, and their shared parent of moral realism, because, as Moore asserted, humans still seem to have an acute, almost intuitive awareness, at least in the abstract, of what we have no choice but to call "right" or "wrong," or the objective truthfulness of some moral properties.

Moral realism begat ethical naturalism, which begat ethical non-naturalism, which in turn begat another variant called ethical intuitionism. The latter seeks to address the innate problem in ethical non-naturalism, called the epistemological problem. Epistemology is the study into the nature of knowledge, and the problem is that if it's impossible to know if anything is good or bad, then it's also potentially impossible to distinguish good from bad. And if we can't do that, then how can we justify any moral actions or principles? Intuition is naturally a major part of ethical intuitionism, and it assumes that humans have a special ability called moral intuition that intrinsically tells each and every one of us what moral properties are truths—it's that sense of right and wrong that leads to moral judgments or actions. Put another way, this is our conscience.

G.E. Moore (1873–1958)

Moore spent most of his career writing and teaching at the University of Cambridge, and he was a contemporary and coworker of more well-known philosophers like Ludwig Wittgenstein and Bertrand Russell. The era when all three were teaching at the same institution has been referred to as "the golden age of Cambridge philosophy."

ANTIREALISM

As moral realism argues that there are many objective moral values, moral antirealism, also called moral irrealism, is the metaethical viewpoint that argues just the opposite: that there are no objectively, independently truthful moral values whatsoever. Antirealism is a large umbrella that encompasses a variety of philosophy styles and ethical schools of thought. For example, it can be used to deny that moral properties even exist, as well as the notion that they do exist, albeit dependent on individual interpretation and usage, and are wholly dependent on humans and their actions.

There are quite a few subsets and sub-subsets of moral antirealism. They include:

- **Ethical subjectivism.** This theory argues that moral statements can only be made true or false by the attitude or viewpoint of an outside observer. This means that interpretation can't help but cloud the objective nature of a moral statement.
- **Moral relativism.** In this school, a morally correct ideal becomes that way via the approval of a society. This can be expanded to mean then that different societies have different ethical standards—again, this suggests that there are no innately moral absolutes.
- **Divine command theory.** A thing becomes "right" or "good" if it is divinely ordained to be so. This is where religion and ethics intersect—adherents of this theory believe in a supernatural deity as the arbiter of good and bad.
- **Individualist subjectivism.** Not only does each society or culture have its own moral standards, but according to this theory, every human on earth follows their own sliding scale as to what constitutes "good" or "bad" behavior.
- **Ideal observer theory.** This theory supposes the opinion of a hypothetical, idealized observer. This observer is rational and capable of perfect reasoning, and a given action is judged by this observer to determine if the act is moral or not. Would this observer approve of an action? If it's "by the book," as it were, then yes, the action is moral.

Chapter 6

EASTERN MORAL PHILOSOPHIES

In the Western tradition, ethics is viewed as a subgenre of the larger, broader field of philosophy proper. Ethics describes ways that we can practically apply (theoretically) universal principles to the situations of everyday life. Because of the predominant Judeo-Christian ethic in Europe and the Americas, philosophy has had to contend with religion for space in academic and mental spheres. More or less, philosophy has been an outgrowth of faith, and for hundreds of years philosophers in Europe and the Americas either willingly or forcibly tried to reconcile their ideas about man's true nature with what their religions had told them was true about God, the universe, and human nature.

But in the vastly large parts of the world collectively referred to as the East, which includes India, China, Japan, and the Middle East, quite the opposite is true. In the East, religion sprang from philosophy. For example, Buddhism is viewed as a major world religion, but it's really a spiritual system and life plan based around the teachings of a man known as the Buddha, a philosopher who was not immortal or divine, but a man who was thought to have unlocked the secrets of the universe. Taoism is also a spiritual system, not a religion, based on the ideas that opposite forces control everything, and that change is always happening and we ought to accept it and live within that framework.

There are more differences between Western and Eastern philosophies, of course. In some ways, the philosophies that came out of the East are more "pure" than Western philosophies, in that, theoretically, Eastern philosophies can be seen as approaching truth without the burden, competition, and shadows of politicized religion that bog down things in the Western world.

Eastern philosophies are also much older than Western philosophies, and it's interesting to see how key concepts in Western philosophy developed completely independently from Eastern philosophical forms. People are people, after all. We all have the same questions, regardless of where or when we're from. In this light, perhaps there are indeed objective truths that can be discovered about ethics and morality.

In this chapter, we'll be looking at the philosophical contributions of some of the most important thinkers in the ancient East, and especially how those contributions are applied in the form of ethics or moral philosophy. It's worth noting that many of these thinkers developed, honed, and spread their theories and wrote them down more than 1,000 years ago.

BUDDHIST ETHICS

Suffering and Noble Truths

In the West, ethical systems have derived from religions, such as the Greek pantheistic system, or the monotheistic worldview of Christianity and Judaism. In the East, religions such as Taoism and especially Buddhism derived from moral and ethical systems. Buddhism isn't even a religion, it's more of an organized system of ethics, a way of life, and a "spiritual tradition" that guides people to ultimate truths, understanding, and enlightenment, which is also called nirvana.

The founder of Buddhism is a man from Nepal formerly known as Siddhartha Gautama (ca. 563–483 B.C.). Years of intense study, meditation, and reflection transformed him into the Buddha, a word in the ancient Indian language of Sanskrit that means "enlightened one." But "Buddha" or "the Buddha" almost always refers to *this* Buddha, such is his influence on spirituality, philosophy, and ethics.

Reaching Nirvana

Nirvana is often used interchangeably with "enlightenment" or "peace," but it's much more than that. Nirvana is a profound transformation to the next level of spiritual consciousness in which the mind discovers its true identify of being infinite and eternal, and that the material world is but a hollow illusion.

Buddhism developed in South Asia and spread throughout the continent over the centuries in part because it presents such an aggressively human approach for how to live well. During the time

Buddha was alive, a movement called *sramana* was common. This was an ascetic movement that advocated the active rejection and shunning of all earthly pleasures, if not self-punishment. In contrast to that, and in answer to an everyday life of too many earthly pleasures, the Buddha came up with the moderate, thoughtful, Middle Way, which is the spiritual path casually referred to today as Buddhism.

THE FOUR NOBLE TRUTHS

At the core of Buddhism is a proclamation and acceptance of the Four Noble Truths. All of the Buddha's teachings can essentially be boiled down to these four profound talking points, which invite as many questions as they answer:

- Life is suffering
- Suffering arises from attachment to desires
- Suffering ceases when attachment to desire ceases
- Freedom from suffering is possible by practicing the Noble Eightfold Path

Adherents to the Noble Eightfold Path to enlightenment, or nirvana, are expected to follow these eight abstract guidelines. These guidelines describe virtues for leading an ethical life, which is then the path to the right way and a life of enlightenment. The entire basis of Buddhism isn't just a series of edicts but a description of several specifically ethics-related principles. The Buddha, after years of study, contemplation, and meditation, created this eight-part method. This method is quite literally the Middle Way, and it sets Buddhism apart from other spiritual and ethical traditions.

THE NOBLE EIGHTFOLD PATH

The eight steps are grouped into themes. The first two steps on the Noble Eightfold Path lead to the cultivation of wisdom.

- **Right view:** Take on the Buddhist viewpoint about life. This includes the concepts that actions have consequences, death is not the end of life, and that the actions in one life affect that of the other.
- **Right resolve:** Dedicate one's life, body, mind, and soul to the pursuit of nirvana.

The next three steps on the Noble Eightfold Path involve how to live out these ethical instructions and requirements.

- **Right speech:** Words matter, and they can harm and hurt. To practice right speech means to refrain from lying, deception, gossip, and chitchat. Buddha believed in speaking only when necessary, and with honest, carefully chosen words that promote love and growth.
- **Right action:** More or less, this is a conscious, considerate living out of the Five Precepts of Buddhism (see the following). Right action means to behave so as not to harm, or to harm as little as possible, a sentient being in any way, be it physically, emotionally, or spiritually. (The old story about a Buddhist monk who won't even harm an insect? That's an example of living out this step on the Noble Eightfold Path.)
- **Right livelihood:** One should be ethical in one's profession, and make one's living in a peaceful, unharmful way. Buddha specifically named four careers that ought to be avoided entirely, because

they bring about nothing but added pain to the universe: dealing weapons, dealing with living things (which includes slavery, the sex trade, and animal slaughter), meat production, and being involved in the manufacture or sale of poisons or intoxicants.

The final three steps on the Noble Eightfold Path lead toward greater development of the mind.

- **Right effort:** An individual must actively try his best, and with all his energy, might, and will, to develop and cultivate a clean and clear state of consciousness and openness.
- **Right mindfulness:** An individual has to put aside earthly and superficial desires so as to allow the mind to be aware and resolute, and to not be distracting by fleeting emotions or changing mental states.
- **Right concentration:** Also called *Samadhi,* it's a commitment to actively focusing and then maintaining one's thoughts on achieving a place of clarity and enlightenment.

THE FIVE PRECEPTS

The Five Precepts handed down by the Buddha are core virtues that can direct a person onto the path of enlightenment. These virtues are expressed as mantras, or prayers. Buddhists are forever training themselves to abide by the practices described in these mantras. These practices are certainly not ones restricted just to Buddhism, although a Buddhist recites these mantras daily as a reminder of them. Adherents chant these mantras either in the original Sanskrit or in their native tongue.

- **Don't kill.** *Panatipata veramani sikkhapadam samadiyami*, or "I undertake the precept to refrain from destroying living creatures."
- **Don't steal.** *Adinnadana veramani sikkhapadam samadiyami*, or "I undertake the precept to refrain from taking that which is not given."
- **Be chaste.** *Kamesu micchacara veramani sikkhapadam samadiyami*, or "I undertake the precept to refrain from sexual misconduct."
- **Speak well and choose your words carefully.** *Musavada veramani sikkhapadam samadiyami*, or "I undertake the precept to refrain from incorrect speech." (This concept is so important to ethical development in Buddhism that it's included in the Noble Eightfold Path as well as the Five Precepts.)
- **Stay away from drugs and alcohol.** *Sura-meraya-majja pamadatthana veramani sikkhapadam samadiyami*, or "I undertake the precept to refrain from intoxicating drinks and drugs which lead to carelessness."

There is no overarching divine figure in Buddhism, not even the Buddha. There's only the universe, life, you, and the goal to reach nirvana. Instead of a god, there's just a general law of the universe that states that some behaviors lead to enlightenment and others bring about suffering. If a behavior brings you closer to enlightenment, it's ethical. If a behavior brings suffering, then it's not ethical. Fortunately there are the Four Noble Truths, Noble Eightfold Paths, and Five Precepts to help make ethical decisions a lot easier.

CONFUCIANISM AND ETHICS

The Interplay of Jen and Li

Kong Qiu, known in the West under the Latinized form of his name Confucius, was a philosopher born in China in 551 B.C. Confucius wrote aphorisms and ethical models for everything from family life to public life to educational systems. One of most broad and all-encompassing philosophical and ethical frameworks bears his name: Confucianism.

WHAT IS JEN?

Two of the basic concepts of Confucianism are called *jen* and *li*. Jen is the idea that humans are made distinctively human by an innate, natural goodness. Confucius himself said that jen was the main human virtue or "the virtue of virtues," and that any and all other virtues are an outgrowth of this one. It's telling though, and in line with other difficult to quantify and difficult to universalize concepts of ethics across the board, that Confucius never gave a specific definition of jen, merely characterizing and describing it in practice. To Confucius, jen, and all its attendant qualities, is more important than life itself. In other words, it is more important for us to maintain the ethical, natural standard of humans, that innate goodness, than it is to pursue one's own personal fulfillment. In this regard, jen is quite similar to the Western philosophical concept of "the greater good."

Jen gives dignity to human life, and this plays out in two ways. The first is that jen drives humans to be kind to other humans—thus it's a natural imperative to be kind. The other is also just as natural:

jen provides self-esteem for the individual, which in turns leads that person to commit moral acts. Confucianism also teaches that there isn't a set amount of jen in any one person, nor is it the same in everyone. Indeed, everyone has some natural human goodness in them, but some have more than others.

However, it is possible to obtain more jen, as Confucius also taught of our ability to obtain perfection (or at least something close to that). How does one get more jen, and thus become more perfect? To find jen, and peace, and goodness, it is more ethical to reject the notion of satisfying one's needs and desires and work instead at bringing kindness and goodness to others. Therefore, the predominant motivator of human action, or the first principle of Confucianism, is to act according to jen, and to seek to extend jen to others. This increases the jen of others and also one's own jen. Confucius realized that a well-ordered culture or society was necessary in order for jen to be expressed or shared.

WHAT IS LI?

This is where the other major aspect of Confucianism, li, comes in. Li is the guide of human action that leads to gains, benefits, and a stable, pleasant order of things. Li is the system or moral framework by which one can share and spread jen.

Confucius broke down the system of li into several "senses," the first being the First Sense, or a guide to human relationships, or how humans ought to interact with one another in the most moral way possible. (In other words, "propriety.") Propriety is all about people being open and kind to one another; it is about focusing on positive words and actions rather than negative ones—which is to say choosing good concrete moral acts instead of actively choosing bad ones. And what is, exactly, a good way to act, so as to be the most kind and pass on the most jen in a gentle way? Confucius called that the Law of the Mean, or "the middle." For Confucius, the most moral choice often meant that one should aim to shoot right down the middle so as to maximize happiness for all.

THE FIVE RELATIONSHIPS

Another element of the First Sense of li is "The Five Relationships." Again, this is the way that Confucius argues things ought to be done, in accordance with maximizing jen. In this regard, the Five Relationships show us how to take the best moral actions in social interactions with friends and family. But these are specific actions, rather than universal actions, as Confucius has broken down all human engagements into one of five categories. They are:

- **Father and son.** The father should be loving to his boy, the boy ought to be reverential to his father.
- **Elder brother and younger brother.** The elder brother should be gentle to his young brother, while the younger brother needs to be respectful to his older sibling.
- **Husband and wife.** A husband is to be "good" to his wife. A wife should "listen" to her husband.
- **Older friend and younger friend.** The older should be considerate of the younger, and the younger should be deferential to the older.
- **Ruler and subject.** Rulers ought to be kind and just. Subjects in turn should and must be loyal.

The idea of age factors into almost all five relationships. This is a concept called "respect for the age," as Confucius wrote that age—and by extension, life experience—gives value and wisdom to lives, institutions, and even objects.

THE CONCEPT OF YI

Confucius gave a name to the natural sense of humans to go and be good: *yi*. It is necessary to have yi to have jen. Yi is a natural sense that humans get, because they are humans and can think and reason, and more important, feel, the moral sense when something is right or when something is wrong. Yi also includes our natural ability to know the right thing to do in most any circumstance. This isn't a moral wisdom (or *chih*), which can be both learned and natural, but intuition—it's just *there*. You're going to have some sense of right or wrong. How you act is a different matter entirely.

Quotable Voices

"Real knowledge is to know the extent of one's ignorance." —Confucius

Confucianism is, then, a form of deontology, not consequentialism. The acts themselves are good, regardless of intention or consequence. Acting from a sense of yi is very close to the ideal of practicing jen. The reason is, if an action is done for the sake of yi—an innate moral ability to do good—it's the right thing to do. But if an action is done out of a sense of jen, that respect for others and a desire to spread goodness, then the act adds good and moral intention to the already moral act.

IBN SINA'S RECONCILIATION

Where Philosophy Meets Theology

Ibn Sina, also known as Avicenna (ca. 980–1037), was a Persian philosopher, physician, and academic. He lived during what in the Islamic world is known as the Golden Age (known in the West as the medieval era). During this time there were great advances in math, science, literature, and more, thanks to people like Ibn Sina. In addition to being a major figure in the history of the study of ethics, he's also regarded as the father of early modern medicine. He had his own system of logic, known in the West as Avicennian logic, as well as the philosophical school of Avicennism.

A Note on Names

It was commonplace for Western printers and scholars to Westernize or Latinize the names of Eastern figures. For example, Ibn Sina was known in the West as Avicenna, which is pronounced almost the same as "Ibn Sina." Another example is Confucius, which is a Latinized version of his real name, Kong Qiu.

There are parallels between Ibn Sina's contributions to philosophy with those of his Western counterparts. For example, as men in the West reconciled a devout Christianity with the exploration of ethical and philosophical concepts, so too did Ibn Sina as a devout Muslim. His philosophies represent major attempts at marrying Islamic theology specifically and monotheism in general with the notions of rationality, free will, and other Platonic and Aristotelian concepts.

THE CHAIN OF EXISTENCE

Ibn Sina was born around the year 980 in Afshana, then part of Persia in what is now the nation of Uzbekistan. He was the son of a scholar and high-ranking government official, who educated him at home. By the age of ten, Ibn Sina had memorized scores of Arabic poetry and the Qur'an. He was studying medicine at thirteen, mastered it at sixteen, and started treating patients (for free) because he loved the study of it so much.

He wrote about 450 treatises on many subjects. More than 200 survive, of which 150 were about philosophy and 40 were of his actual life's work in medicine. (Among them are *The Book of Healing*, a philosophical and scientific encyclopedia.) He explored and really helped define Islamic philosophy when the religion was relatively young—the founder of Islam, Muhammad, lived in the 600s, and Ibn Sina was working just 300 years later. As a prominent member of society, he had access to the works of Aristotle, which he read and critiqued, or rather "corrected." His philosophies reconcile Aristotelianism, as well as Neoplatonism, with theology.

Here's what he determined: the universe is made of a chain of physical beings, and each being on the chain brings about existence for the being directly below on the chain—stretching from God to angels to the souls of humans. But he also said an infinite chain was impossible, and so the chain had to terminate in a simple, self-efficient being that, via the chain, contained an essence of God and all the spiritual beings above it. In other words, humans were this last link in the chain. This is philosophically interesting because he rationalized out the existence of God, although the argument only works within its own logic and falls apart when exposed to outside scrutiny.

AVICENNIAN LOGIC

Avicennian logic was an alternative to Aristotelian logic, and was the dominant system in Islamic institutions by the twelfth century. It spread to Europe as well. He developed a concept called *tabula rasa*, Latin for "blank slate." It's the concept that human beings are born empty—with no innate or preexisting mental impressions. This concept predates the nature versus nurture argument, though it comes down hard on the side of nurture. Even though we are essentially divine, Avicenna reasoned, we must be shaped in a way so as to utilize and express that divinity.

During a spell in prison after a dispute with a local leader whom he wouldn't assist, Avicenna developed a thought experiment called Floating Man. It showed that humans are self-aware and that the soul is real. The idea was this: Imagine yourself suspended in air, isolated from sensations, as if you're in a sensory deprivation tank. You still have self-consciousness, and thus you are "proving" that the self isn't logically dependent on a physical form. The soul, therefore, unlike knowledge or sensations, is a primary or "given" thing.

Quotable Voices

"There are no incurable diseases, only the lack of will. There are no worthless herbs, only the lack of knowledge." —Ibn Sina

Not unlike Western philosophers grappling with Christianity and how it fit in to broader philosophical concepts, Islamic ethics came from a study and questioning of religious tenets such as *qadar* (predetermination), *taklif* (obligation), and the exploitation of the people by unjust caliphs, or Muslim rulers. But Ibn Sina developed a theory of the meeting of the soul with the active intellect. This theory is bound up as the ultimate perfection of the soul, attaining the highest degree of wisdom as well as virtue. The active intellect is similar to free will or rationality in that it is the tool by which ethical agents act, and so therefore make the world go 'round. Man can achieve enlightenment or happiness while still mortal, but that enlightenment is defined as being a mirror of the higher up intelligible, divine world in which humanity is the final link in the chain.

IBN MISKAWAYH AND AL-GHAZALI

Major Middle Eastern Ethicists

Among the major Golden Age of Islam ethicists from the Middle East was a philosopher named Ahmad ibn Muhammad Ibn Miskawayh, or as he's usually referred to, Ibn Miskawayh (ca. 932–1030). He wrote a book called *Cultivation of Morals*, among other things, which started the tradition of Persian ethics. As was often the case with early Islamic ethics writing, the basis for Ibn Miskawayh's theories were ideas laid down by Plato that had spread to the East. For example, Plato wrote about the division of the soul into three areas: appetites for pleasures and comforts, our sense of righteous anger, and our conscious and rational sense of awareness. Similarly, Ibn Miskawayh broke the soul—or, as he more closely equated it, one's innate sense of pure humanity that leads to moral action—into multiple parts.

INNATE VIRTUES OF THE SOUL

What Ibn Miskawayh called parts of the soul, Western philosophers called virtues. The first part of the soul is the virtue of wisdom, which represents the rational part of the soul and the sense that it is important or desirable to act in a morally correct way. The second part consists of courage. The third part is justice, which Ibn Miskawayh believed was a form of moderation or proportion. However, that third part—justice—only occurs (and leads the soul to a place of harmony and ethical awareness) when the other two parts are engaged. In other words, in order to act morally (and to feel good about it) and be justified, individuals must want to act in a moral way in which they are morally inclined. They must feel it vitally necessary to act, and feel fulfilled afterward that the decision was right and just and helpful. In terms of relating to Plato, each part relates to the Platonic trinity. Plato's appetites corresponded to Ibn Miskawayh's desire to be moral. Righteous anger corresponds to the virtue of courage. And one's rational, deeply felt awareness to justice corresponds to the outward act of justice. The similarities to Greek thought end there. Aristotle wrote that when that trinity was in effect, it led to virtues, virtuous deeds, and virtuous thoughts. As far as Ibn Miskawayh was concerned, this was the essence, foundation, and whole of virtue.

Ibn Miskawayh further subdivided his notion of internal moral justice: Justice is such a high virtue that it must have divine involvement. The supreme virtue of justice must be couched by adhering to God's law, or shari'a. God extends the responsibility of justice to imams (Muslim leaders) and caliphs in order to send the praise for the justice and union of the soul back to God, where it belongs. Ibn Miskawayh also borrows substantially from Neoplatonic thinkers in his notion and expression of happiness. Theoretical happiness to him occurs only in conjunction with an engaged and morally active intellect, or a well-used rationality, thus propelling the individual to a realm of higher intellectualism, and thus happiness.

AL-GHAZALI

Ibn Miskawayah inspired several ethicists in his wake, chief among them Al-Ghazali (1058–1111). In works like *The Balance of Action* and *The Revival of the Religious Sciences*, Al-Ghazali expanded on Ibn Miskawayah's ideas and took them to their logical conclusion.

This is to say he developed a psychologically grounded, ethical framework built on Platonic ideas that maintained an Islamic worldview, along with a fair amount of mysticism.

Al-Ghazali laid out the same four cardinal virtues that Plato stated were of utmost importance: courage, temperance, wisdom, and justice (this also corresponds with the parts of the soul that Ibn Miskawayah wrote about). But Al-Ghazali doesn't leave them alone on their pedestal, but rather he adds in some religious ethics–building in order to create a morally correct path by which happiness can be obtained.

Quotable Voices

"Declare your jihad on twelve enemies you cannot see: egoism, arrogance, conceit, selfishness, greed, lust, intolerance, anger, lying, cheating, gossiping, and slandering. If you can master and destroy them, then you will be ready to fight the enemy you can see." —Al-Ghazali

Adding in religious ethics–building involves the cardinal virtues and also other, more worldly and tenable virtues. Al-Ghazali suggests that happiness is the main aim, but that there are also two parts of that happiness, or at least two types: worldly and otherworldly. The otherworldly kind of happiness needs worldly goods and temporal things to come about, such as the four cardinal virtues of courage, temperance, wisdom, and justice, but also the bodily virtues of good general health, strength, good fortune (or luck), and longevity. In addition to that are external values: guidance, good advice, direction, and most notably, divine support and guidance (known in the Qur'an as hadith, or in Christianity as the Holy Spirit). It's the whole package of virtues, both realistic and unseen.

All told and all combined, Al-Ghazali's path to moral perfection is one and the same with the individual's quest to become closer to God and become more like God. To find that, two conditions must be met. The first is that divine law must govern one's actions and the intentions behind the actions. The other condition is that God must always be present in the mind and the heart, which is expressed with things like submission, adoration, contrition, and appreciation for the beauty and power of the divine authority.

TAOIST ETHICS

The Yin and the Yang

Many ethical theories take for granted that humans are imbued with some kind of ethical code. Other theories hold that there's some kind of divine or universal law that objectively states what things are moral and what things are not. The entire history of moral philosophy has been built by philosophers who were trying to use reason to decipher just how much of ethics is natural, how much of it is nurture, and how we can get closer to those truths by adopting certain virtues or treating one another in a moral, ethically just way.

But what if all of that is contrived, artificial, forced, and ultimately unnatural and thus completely stifling to the human spirit and our sense of individuality and integrity? This is the starting point of the Chinese spiritual tradition of Taoism, which dates back to around the fourth century B.C. Western theories push against our sometimes natural inclination to do bad things (and these inclinations must be natural, because we *do* do bad things, whether we know better or not). Western philosophy favors a constant cultivation of virtue and the constant getting-to-the-meat of moral truths. Taoists reject this, and instead embrace a reimagining of what "natural" means as well as what "virtuous" means.

Ethical programs are always trying to simplify the universe into "good" and "bad" so that moral ideals are easier to follow. Taoism, however, revels in the complex, tricky nature of human behavior.

YIN AND YANG

Taoism is about the interplay, and analysis of, the yin and yang. Put simply, these two forces represent the constant but changing flows that occur naturally in every part of life. These opposites can be defined in any number of ways, but Taoism is literally a black-and-white way of looking at things. Indeed, Taoism is a way of accepting both the black and the white of things without rejecting or excluding anything that doesn't fit into its structures. In Taoism the *relationship* between the yin and yang is at the core of the philosophy, not just the yin or just the yang. For example, goodness is a part of life, but so is evil. There is pleasure, and there is pain, and they exist only in relation to each other. Such is life—interconnected and interdependent relationships where those two opposing forces are always at play.

The progenitors of Taoism might have believed that the usual, traditional, normative ethical theories of the West were bogged down with strict rules and guidelines as they pertained to virtues and principles that must always be followed. To them this process would have seemed, as is often the case with Western thought, extremely linear. Taoists believed in a better way, or the way of the tao.

Tao simply means "the way." Which way? Not some expert like Plato's way or Kant's way, but *the* way, the way that was around long before those guys. According to Taoism, the way is nature's way. But of course, it's difficult to understand nature's way, as that's really what all moral philosophers are trying to do.

THE WAY

You've probably seen the *taijitu* before—the yin/yang symbol, the black-and-white circle in which the white (yang) has a black dot and the black (yin) has a white dot. That's a marvelous bit of graphic design for an ancient spiritual path. The two colors represent how there are always two opposing forces and how they interact and connect with each other as a natural part of their trajectory. You'll also notice that the forces are in motion, swirling around and kind of moving into the other, the yin into the yang and the yang into the yin.

This, say Taoists, is how the universe actually works. Nature is composed of a series of opposites, yins and yangs. Nature is also, like the taijitu, always moving, and the yins and yangs are always moving into each other. The universe works in a fluid, interconnected way. One could not exist without the other, nor is one *superior* to the other. And this is how the world works, in many ways. There are many things in life that are quite binary but with lots of movement in between. Cold becomes its opposite, hot, but is warm in between. First you are born and then you die, but there's life in between. As it applies to life, one cannot simply live in a yin and never go toward the yang. Life is in motion, and humans must accept this and behave accordingly.

So if this is how the universe is, what does this mean for ethics? It means that good is not superior to or better than bad, merely that they are two sides of the same coin, and that coin is human behavior. As this is the natural way of the world and everything in it, approaching morality as all good or all evil does not work for a Taoist. There is vice to go along with virtue.

THE VALUE OF TE

This doesn't mean that Taoists hold virtue and vice in the same regard. They just accept that one is going to happen while encouraging and cultivating the other—virtue is definitely the preferable of the two options. As part of the interplay and harmony of ethical principles in Taoism, Taoists believe in the potential of every living thing, called *te*, which also means individual integrity. The Tao is expressed in a unique way in each unique thing, and if Taoists want to live life according to the way, they must live life in a way that comes forth out of their own te. Doing so includes both acting virtuous and interacting in a natural way with the world and others. Or put another way, it means living in harmony.

Who Created Taoism?

Lao-Tzu is regarded as the father of Taoism, as he's historically been credited as the author of the *Tao Te Ching,* the book of Taoism principles and precepts. In the twentieth century, however, many scholars suggested that Lao-Tzu may be a mythical figure, and that the *Tao Te Ching* was compiled by many authors.

Expressing te and living a virtuous and harmonious life means being open to the changing flow of life and experiences. Instead of approaching life with rules that have predetermined what is good and what is evil, a Taoist lives in the moment and goes forth in what the te is telling him or her to do. This allows Taoists to enjoy a more adaptable way of life, such that they are more able to handle decisions on a case-by-case basis. Actions for Taoists aren't shaped by social constructs or rules; rather, they are simply shaped by "the way."

Chapter 7

NEGATIVE VIEWS ON ETHICS

By and large ethics is the study of how and why one should act good. But that's just part of the equation. Ethics seek to quantify and explain human behavior, and despite the presence of true human goodness, one can't deny that people have a dark streak. Some philosophers have explored that darkness and negativity as it relates to ethics. For instance, if being good is part of life, then isn't being "bad" also a part of life? And if it's natural to be selfish or cruel, then could it also be considered *ethical* to be selfish or cruel? Some philosophers went down this road, as did others who explored the ethical ramifications of the possibility that humanity exists apart from any sort of moral or divine framework whatsoever.

- **Niccolò Machiavelli.** In the sixteenth century he urged people to use ethics to manipulate others and strive at all costs to obtain and keep power, often ruthlessly. Why? Because it is in our nature to do so.
- **Jean-Paul Sartre.** He was a twentieth-century proponent of existentialism, or the idea that life has no innate meaning and man has no true purpose. This lack of predetermination means that all humans have freedom and choice, and utter and complete free will to live a life as they see fit on their own terms.

- **Friedrich Nietzsche.** This nineteenth-century German philosopher wrote about man's duty to create life in one's own image—to make oneself as great and varied a person as possible, and to reject traditions and institutions along the way, for they were outdated and held back true moral growth.
- **Arthur Schopenhauer.** Diverging from most all other moral philosophers, this early nineteenth-century philosopher thought that the universe is an essentially irrational place, which has major consequences on how humans behave ethically.
- **Ludwig Wittgenstein.** An important twentieth-century philosopher, he called all of moral philosophy into question by questioning the veracity of the one real tool philosophers have at the ready: their words.

NICCOLÒ MACHIAVELLI

The Darker Side of Ethics

Niccolò Machiavelli (1469–1527) represents the dark, under-handed, and manipulative side of moral philosophy. In seminal works like *The Prince*, Machiavelli explored how ethics can be used for personal means to an end, particularly as a way to obtain and keep fame, power, and money by any means necessary. He is under-standably a controversial philosopher, but not an unpopular one, because he focused on the darker, undeniable side of human nature that many ethicists choose to ignore or believe can be worked out of a person.

Machiavelli lived in the city-state of Florence during Renais-sance Italy, and served as a diplomat in the early 1500s. By 1512, Florence was under the control of the rich and powerful Medici family, and as part of the old guard, he was tried for treason and exiled. In 1513 he wrote *The Prince*, and, taking a bit of his own advice on the tricks to get what he wanted, he dedicated it to Lorenzo de' Medici. The trick to win favor didn't work, but the book has since become a de facto handbook for calculating movers and shakers. What's scary is that he wrote *The Prince* as a how-to guide for public figures, politicians, and others who wanted to get an upper hand on others and obtain power. The term *Machiavel-lian* refers to scheming, power-crazed kinds of behaviors because Machiavelli himself told people it was not only ethical to behave this way, per the reasoning of his argument, but that they simply must.

SERVE THYSELF

In an overarching sense, Machiavelli is a consequentialist. Writing in the early 1500s, he was one of the first to explore the notion that actions should be judged solely in terms of their consequences, which is to say, what one can gain from them. However, Machiavelli departed from other consequentialist thinkers because he was not concerned with the resulting happiness for others, or the moral fortitude of the action, the agent, or the consequences. The only thing Machiavelli said to worry about is yourself. Like a consequentialist, Machiavelli didn't judge an action because some divine order from a god said the action was moral, or because that action was born out of a cherished virtue. Machiavelli was concerned only with the end result, which is getting power, holding on to that power, and keeping that power—at any cost.

In Machiavellian ethics, the individual's grab for power is, technically speaking, ethical. That means that the actions that lead to that end are also ethical, even though they may appear cold, callous, calculating, or cruel to others.

Quotable Voices

"The wise man does at once what the fool does finally." —Niccolò Machiavelli

Clearly, Machiavelli didn't think too highly of humans. Specifically, he thought we retained all the nastiness of animals but had been gifted the ability to reason—and scheme. Humans, he wrote, are depraved, cruel, heartless, and selfish, and we ought to just accept those things as being real and innate. In the language of ethics, because those negative qualities are innate, they are thereby "good." This is to say, these negative qualities are virtues. And one should use these virtues (or anti-virtues) to get what they, and only they, want out of life and others.

Of course this philosophy influences how one should treat people—by exploiting them in any way possible so as to get closer to the goal, whatever it may be. And because everyone is grabbing for power, everyone is looking for opportunities to best everyone else. Trust no one, Machiavelli said, because your neighbors, coworkers, and friends are just like you. They, like you, are after the power and they, like you, are willing and ready to step all over you to get it. For example, in *The Prince*, Machiavelli argues for breaking the rules, even moral rules, because such rule breaking was a way to gain and hold power over others. ("Politics," he once wrote, "have no relation to morals.") He advocated breaking contracts if doing so was of personal benefit, because that other person just might break the contract with you if it suited his or her wicked nature. He advised us to treat everything like a tool, and to make judgments on a black-and-white moral basis: something is a "good" tool if it helps you achieve your goals, and it's a "bad" tool if it doesn't, or allows others to gain power over you.

JEAN-PAUL SARTRE AND EXISTENTIALISM

Good News, Nothing Matters

Some philosophers say we should look to broad societal indications to learn what's moral. Others say there are innate truths about what is and is not moral. Others say human nature is innately a good one, and that this determines our drives to be moral and reflects our virtues. But what if none of those is the case? What if humans, both collectively as a race and individually at birth, are a blank slate with no kind of inclination whatsoever? This is the main moral center of the radical philosophy of existentialism, as best represented by French writer Jean-Paul Sartre (1905–1980).

EXTREME PERSONAL RESPONSIBILITY

Most would agree, at least on some level, with the existentialist idea that people are responsible, entirely, for not only what they already are but what they will ultimately be. Existentialism holds that this determination includes if a person is going to be moral or virtuous. The key term here is "going to be," because nothing is predetermined. At all. Those morals and virtues are entirely up to the individual, and beyond that, however one chooses to define it. Happiness doesn't derive from preexisting virtues, or if it does, it's because a person chose to live a traditionally virtuous life and he does so at his pleasure. It's entirely up to the individual. Neither other people nor the universe nor any external force can be blamed for unhappiness, because in existentialism, all ideas are decisions that come from within. Sartre says that much of what we mistake for moral behavior is just our need to get along with others so that we can keep things civil. The need to keep things civil indicates a lack of moral courage. Without it, an individual can't be true to oneself or live an authentic life, and is instead constantly manipulated by external factors.

On Existentialism

Existentialism enjoys a reputation as an extraordinarily negative, pessimistic, or even sad philosophy. This could be true, as it attests that "life is meaningless." But this is merely a response to organized religion; if Christianity gives life meaning because there's a God at its center and heaven is a reward for good behavior, then in existentialism, yes, life is meaningless because there is no great creator, guiding deity, or promise of an afterlife paradise. However, this lack of predetermination gives humankind—and each human—absolutely limitless freedom and choice.

ALONE IN THE UNIVERSE

Sartre affirms that humans have no innate nature. We are thrown into the world of someone else's making and thus have to figure out our place. He writes that "existence precedes essence." In other words, we exist, and then we choose what we are. There is nothing innate—there is only what we ultimately choose to be. We are not held to any kind of moral standard or divine or natural law. There is none of that, and so this philosophy offers us a special kind of freedom. Indeed it is an overwhelming freedom, in that each of us must figure out how to live life completely on our own. We are, as Sartre says, "a plan aware of itself." Through our own choices, he is saying, we determine or create the ideal moral human by figuring out what that ideal is, and then acting it out. Since you choose what sort of person you should be, it's your responsibility to create yourself in that ideal. That's a lot of pressure, but it means you can choose whatever you want your virtues to be. And it serves as a model for the way everyone should choose.

Quotable Voices

"Man is condemned to be free; because once thrown into the world, he is responsible for everything he does." —Jean-Paul Sartre

Anguish results when we deny ourselves the responsibility of creating our ideal self and go along with others. Such denial is self-deception or bad faith. Being forlorn comes from abandoning the idea that we are our only source of value. There's a certain amount of despair in being alone in the universe, in there being no reward, grand plan, or afterlife. Sartre writes that humans are, after all, condemned to be free.

Sartre never published a book outlining his specific ethical views or virtues. And why would he? He had his virtues, and you have yours. In this way, he was the ultimate relativist.

THE ETHICS OF FRIEDRICH NIETZSCHE

From Man to Superman

While he did write in the nineteenth century, German philosopher, writer, and philology professor Friedrich Nietzsche (1844–1900) was among the first "contemporary philosophers." Writing about timeless absolutes, the origins of ethics, and critiquing and expanding upon the work of other philosophers from hundreds of years earlier didn't interest Nietzsche quite as much as the emerging modern society. Industrialization was rapidly transforming the world as it moved headlong into the twentieth century, and Nietzsche was fascinated with the philosophical and ethical underpinnings of modern civilization and his contemporary world. In his writings, he sought to tear down long-held, traditional ideas about ethics and human nature.

He held that a commitment to one's own integrity requires living a life that aims to acquire power and express inner strength. To do that means a person must strive, passionately and always, to live life in his own way. He believed an individual should set his own moral code, apart from what everybody else was doing, because everyone else was doing just that.

STRIKING OUT ON ONE'S OWN

Successfully living in your own way requires determining your own interpretation of life, and then taking on new and diverse experiences in hopes of actually challenging your own interpretation. One must have a fluid view of the world to have a more fluid inner life, which in turn will cultivate a rich, sophisticated, and singular interpretation of how to live life.

Nietzsche's philosophy, however, is in opposition to traditional ethics—or at least to how traditional ethics had been presented and discussed up to the nineteenth century. He said that the traditional ways of determining ethics left little room for the creation and cultivation of the individual. In fact, he determined that that was a fatal flaw of ethics: in trying to determine universal truths about how everyone ought to be and behave, philosophers focused too heavily on the overarching principles, and this created a herd mentality. By and large, ethical systems of the past did very little analysis of the development of the individual on that person's own terms—merely they looked at the way an individual ought to fall in line and have the same strictures and principles as everyone else. The guidelines to be like everyone else (in the name of harmony and the pursuit of happiness) resulted in what Nietzsche said caused mass conformity to interpretations of life that had been created by some stranger long ago. And that was not okay.

Ethics can become so internalized, Nietzsche argued, that they can actually harm you. But there is a way out, and it is for the individual to work his way out of the ethical codes that have been deeply ingrained by culture and rearing. Nietzsche asserted that virtuous behavior can't be separated from the individual. This is, however, a form of deontology, in that ethics should not focus on what a person actually does (or the consequences of those actions) but on the moral fortitude that motivates that person. This is getting into the "good intentions make all the difference" method of ethics, but in Nietzsche's reading it means that if ethics are beyond strict categorizations and are left up to billions of different motivations in billions of different people, then there are a lot more pathways in life that are possible—and perfectly morally correct—than simply "good" or "bad." An acceptance of the possibility of multiple pathways can lead to integrity.

CREATING A NEW SENSE OF SELF

For Nietzsche the road to a life of integrity is paved with expressing one's individuality, or creating oneself. That doesn't necessarily mean recreating one's personality in his own image, but it could. What he meant was that people should always be looking for—and taking on—new ways with which to enrich their lives. Doing this means being passionate, learning new things, and trying new experiences so as to gain sophistication, knowledge, wisdom, and understanding. It leads an individual to have a better understanding of life, of the world, and helps a person create an interpretation of the world on his or her own terms. As such, one does do not need to have these things dictated by a religion (which are flawed, corrupted, and outdated, according to Nietzsche) or an ethical system or even one's own past interpretations. Nietzsche believed the mind and spirit, for lack of a unifying word, should never be at rest, but should always be in a place of challenge and flux. Doing this, however, requires a great deal of virtues. To step out of one's comfort zone and try things takes inner strength, power, courage, and resolve—virtues all. To that end, in 1883 he wrote about the Übermensch, or "superman." Nietzsche's ideal was a person who was so dedicated to self-improvement and perfection that he transcended labels, even that of man. This ideal man becomes instead a superman, a near-perfect being of his own creation.

"GOD IS DEAD"

Nietzsche's most famous quote, and the inspiration for a lot of what would later be called existentialism, was found in his 1882 book *The Gay Science*. A character named the madman says, "God is dead. God remains dead. And we have killed him. How shall we, the murderers of murderers, console ourselves?" Nietzsche doesn't really mean that the actual being of God, the Christian God, is dead. He is trying to say that humans can better serve their individuality and self-creation by rejecting their past notions of "God." Or religion. Or ethical frameworks. Why? Because it's simply too easy to just blame God for things, because to not think or explore the reasons for things can lead to an unchallenged life, which Nietzsche was decidedly against. With God dead, individuals can take charge of their own lives on their own terms. It's scary, but that's where the inner virtues come into play.

Quotable Voices

"On the mountains of truth you can never climb in vain: either you will reach a point higher up today, or you will be training your powers so that you will be able to climb higher tomorrow." —Friedrich Nietzsche

THE PHILOSOPHIES OF ARTHUR SCHOPENHAUER

East + West = Pessimism

Among the few Western philosophers to draw on the Eastern tradition, rather than just to expound on the Western philosophers who came before, was Arthur Schopenhauer (1788–1860). Born in Poland, Schopenhauer married Buddhist principles with Western philosophical concepts, especially those of Immanuel Kant. One of his theories was the idea that no experiences are universal, because we can only experience things as they appear or seem to us; that the world is never as it actually is. He asserted that, as the Buddhists believe, the world is an unknowable illusion.

Quotable Voices

"The more unintelligent a man is, the less mysterious existence seems to him."
—Arthur Schopenhauer

The concept of acknowledging and accepting that there is naturally going to be pain and suffering in life isn't something Schopenhauer made up. It's firmly rooted in two Eastern philosophical traditions: Buddhism and Taoism. Buddhism calls for an acceptance of suffering as a part of life, while Taoism describes the constant interplay of positive and negative forces, and how life is made up of the movement between the two. Another thing Schopenhauer expanded on from Buddhism is the idea that the world, or rather all that we can experience and thus know, is an illusion. We don't really know the world; we can only know that which we can see and experience through our own perspectives, which is invariably going to be a subjective distortion of reality according to our wants and needs.

MASTER OF THE UNIVERSE

All that can be experienced and understood, including ethical ideals, is part of one's representation of reality. This is the ultimate in subjectivity, in saying that the world is unknowable, only one's idea of it, and that everything must be filtered through this concept. Also, this means that the world isn't really the world at all, because you can't know the world. Rather, the world is your world, and so nothing that isn't part of your representation can enter it. Schopenhauer expands on and departs from Kant in using this subjective view of reality to find a place for the Will (the tool by which you shape this world) as a formative force stronger than the intellect, because it is the Will that has to drive what is now "the world."

Schopenhauer states that our influence on the world is tremendous and all-powerful, in that because you are the master of the world and because you perceive it as only you can, the world is completely what you make of it. Acknowledging this influential power affects not only your opinions and moral judgments but also time, space, your body, and your actions. It is up to you then to find your moral codes. The Will is thus central to the human experience; with the Will humans shape and form everything. Which is to say that nothing is innate, nothing is inherent, at least from person to person. One person chooses his ideas based on his Will; another person chooses her ideas based on her Will; and you choose your ideas based on your Will. There is no objective or innate morality to actions, rules, or agents, or even a situation: morality is merely what you perceive ethics to be in your worldview, which you then make happen with your Will.

THE DILEMMA OF DESIRE

Life being an expression of the Will makes for a goal-oriented life. Because we have the tool of the Will (a hammer) then we are always looking for something to use it on (a nail). This is true for higher-consciousness animals, such as humans. Even as we seek goals, we are not satisfied, and so unfulfilled desires move us forward. And if we don't satisfy that desire, we remain unfulfilled. But once all goals are fulfilled, there can be no more motivation because we are satisfied. If that happens, then what's the point of life? Schopenhauer might point out that the desire for life is motion toward some kind of goal. Without that motion, there is no life. This then is the dilemma of desire, which ties back in with Buddhism, and how suffering is life, and particularly how suffering arises from the attachment to desire. And when someone is unfulfilled and suffering, Schopenhauer suggests, on come the dangers of pessimism.

THE VIRTUES OF PESSIMISM

In his 1819 work *The World as Will and Representation*, Schopenhauer describes another pretty out-there idea: pessimism. More than just a negative outlook on life, Schopenhauer had a view that absolutely everything was ultimately bad. (Such is his prerogative, as that is his Will's formation of the world as he sees it.) Pessimism means to see life in a generally negative way. He had some proof of the world being a terrible place: examples of injustice, disease, pain, suffering, and general cruelty abounded. Buddhism agrees with him, but Buddhism also accepts the positive flow of goodness. But as Sartre argued that existentialism was ultimately freeing (it's not so bad that the world is so bad), Schopenhauer argued that if the world was any worse, it wouldn't exist. That's because existence is futile, as it is characterized by wants and desires that can never be attained.

LUDWIG WITTGENSTEIN AND THE LANGUAGE OF ETHICS

Choose Your Words Wisely

Ludwig Wittgenstein (1889–1951) is among the major twentieth-century philosophers of any style or school. He earned this distinction despite that he wrote just a single seventy-five-page book on the subject, *Tractatus Logico-Philosophicus* (roughly *Logical Philosophical Treatise*). Wittgenstein believed this work to be so devastating to the study of philosophy that he thought he permanently destroyed the discipline entirely, allowing him to retreat into a relatively quiet life of becoming an elementary school teacher in his native Austria. Wittgenstein was certainly a character with a dark streak, befitting that of his philosophical role model, the eternally pessimistic Arthur Schopenhauer. The key to Wittgenstein's observations is that the inherent flaws in human communication don't allow us to fully express ourselves or share the same outlook or observations as anyone else. If we can't come together, Wittgenstein implied, then there can be no universals, and no universal meanings.

One of Wittgenstein's main areas of study was the philosophy of language, including its origins, what it means, how it's used, and how language reflects or doesn't reflect reality. Instead of asking what things mean, Wittgenstein would ask, "What is meaning?" Instead of finding the right words to describe what is true and right, he asked, "How does language reflect reality?"

With *Tractatus Logico-Philosophicus*, Wittgenstein applied his analysis and skepticism of language. His findings: a solution to every major philosophical problem of all time...by means of dissolving philosophical inquiry. (But he was not happy about it; he wrote in the preface that "it shows how little is achieved when these problems are solved.") His primary argument in the treatise was that philosophical issues only ever develop due to misunderstandings because of flaws in language. Wittgenstein held that meaning was related to certain nuances of speech and how things were communicated, not so much to the actual words themselves.

Determining the nature of meaning is not easy to ascertain. Simply put, meaning is information sent from one person to another via verbal or written communication, using a common language. This is broken down into types of meaning: conceptual meaning and associative meaning. Conceptual meaning is the more objective kind, the definitions of words, and associative meaning has to do with how the speaker and the listener uniquely and individually understand those words.

PICTURE THIS

Wittgenstein came up with the "picture theory of meaning" to describe his take. As pictures represent the world visually, language represents the way reality is. But language depictions are not as accurate as picture depictions. A picture *is* a picture, and it captures the physical state of an object in time. Interpretation isn't debatable. Words and communication are different. Humans are able to discuss reality, to a degree, because they have the words to describe it. However, sentence structure and language rules cloud the meaning of the individual words, thus making perfect, true communication of a thought from one person to another virtually impossible. Boiled down, sentences lack meaning because they don't convey truth, and thus language doesn't truly reflect the true state of reality (or even an individual's interpretation thereof).

Wittgenstein nonetheless thought that humans could analyze thoughts and sentences and use better language to express themselves in a more perfect or "true logical form." But he noted that difficult abstract philosophical concepts that are different from one person to the next and based on thoughts and feelings, rather than observable criteria, *cannot* be discussed because there are no universal words to express them. That means, as far as Wittgenstein is concerned, all of philosophy is impossible to discuss because their finer points are inexpressible.

Young Wittgenstein

The nuances of language and speech were important to Wittgenstein at even a young age—after being homeschooled he studied at Realschule in Linz, Austria, in 1903 (alongside classmate Adolf Hitler) and reportedly spoke only in intricate High German, with a stutter, and used formal forms of address with classmates. He's said to have had a hard time fitting in.

However, these observations led Wittgenstein not to entirely abandon philosophy, but to advocate for the adoption of "ordinary language philosophy." That approach, Wittgenstein claimed, would involve using language that was as simple as possible when discussing ethical concepts so that everyone could understand them—because everyone *should* be able to understand the big questions and discuss the big concepts of existence. And yet, in the end, such elements of philosophical study would amount to little more than "language games" and thought exercises—because language's flaws prevent anything more than a superficial dive.

Chapter 8

OTHER MORAL PHILOSOPHERS

As you've by now likely discovered, there are few disciplines as vast, complicated, specific, and yet also interconnected, as ethics. It's also a discipline that spans several thousands of years across multiple continents, with many of the field's major players adding to or detracting from each other's work, or paralleling the work of other, unconnected thinkers from far away. The divergences and overlaps between Eastern philosophy and Western philosophy demonstrate this.

In spite of all of that there are quite a few other moral philosophical theories that don't quite fit in with the major schools of thought. They use the same tools and methods, and even some of the same predecessors as the major ones, but they arrive at completely different ends. That's ethics for you—as individualistic and varied as there are reasons to act ethically. And some incredibly smart thinkers derived ethical notions that stand completely on their own, apart from the other ethical umbrellas.

In this chapter we'll look at some of the iconoclasts, lone wolves, minor theorists, and mavericks that blazed a trail off the beaten path of mainstream ethics. We will discuss the works of:

- **Peter Abelard.** This twelfth-century French philosopher and theologian wrote about many philosophical issues, but his most important contribution to the field of ethics was his notion of nominalism. Abelard noted that the subjective nature of philosophy and language means that it's impossible to have universal ideas about philosophies. And if we all can't agree on what things mean, then how are we to come to some sort of universal objectivity?

- **Voltaire.** The eighteenth-century French academic, playwright, and philosopher advocated hedonism, or the idea that the utmost point in life was to seek pleasure, and for all to seek pleasure, and that it was moral to do so.

- **John Locke.** This seventeenth-century British philosopher was at the forefront of the age of the Enlightenment. He brought new attention to the ethical applications of politics, particularly how an ethical ruler should rule, and the morally underscored social contracts between governments and individuals. He also wrote about the power of education on a morally upright individual.

- **Lord Shaftesbury.** Writing in the early 1700s, this English aristocrat and philosopher popularized moral sense theory, which is the ethical idea that the best way to tell whether an act is moral or immoral is by the nature of the emotional response it provokes.

- **Baruch Spinoza.** This seventeenth-century Dutch philosopher differed from other moral philosophers in their quest to separate and identify the different aspects of universal truth. Spinoza held that God and nature were one and the same, as were the physical and mental realms.

PETER ABELARD AND NOMINALISM

Not All Can Be Explained

If you think the subtle differences between different schools of thought and subtypes of ethics can sometimes amount to minor semantic differences, or a matter of word choice, then you're going to be very interested in the ethical concept of nominalism. It's a doctrine that holds that all the agreed upon terms moral philosophers use as a shorthand to describe the precise concepts of their life's work are merely words. This doesn't mean they mean nothing, merely that there is little to no connection between all of the concepts that govern human behavior and moral purpose and the words used to describe those things. In nominalism, concepts, terms, and universals, as we know them, exist only as the words we've attached to them.

THE TRUTH IS OUT THERE

In nominalism, different things that are "good" or "moral" have no relation to each other, than that they've both been labeled the same thing. Nominalists hold that only physical, quantifiable things can be labeled as real. Owing to the complications and inherently subjective nature of language, there thus can be no universal concepts in ethics, or at least not ones that can be universally understood in the same way by all people.

Moderate Realism

In between Platonic realism and nominalism is moderate realism. The latter holds that while there isn't a separate realm where universal concepts reside, these concepts nonetheless are part of the fiber of our being in space and time, and they exist when they exist. This view is similar to another stopgap solution called conceptualism, which says that universals exist within the mind and not on an external or scientific plane.

Nominalism is a rational, natural response to the overriding goal—but often the problem—of moral philosophy, which is the drive to identify and define universals. Specifically, nominalism is a contrarian outgrowth of Platonic realism, the concept created by the ancient Greek philosopher Plato. In that theory, abstract ideas—such as universal moral truths—do, in fact, exist; and they do so in their own right and are independent of the physical world or humanity's adoption of them. Nominalists may ask exactly what this overriding universal might be and where it is. As this universal doesn't hold up to rational scrutiny, or definition, nominalists are quite skeptical that it exists. And if the universal doesn't exist, neither do its truths. This means that all truths are suspect, simply because the universal cannot be identified, quantified, or explained in an objective, scientific way.

GOOD INTENTIONS, BETTER LUCK

Nominalism is actually quite old, as far as moral philosophy goes. It was likely the creation of a medieval French philosopher and theologian named Roscelin of Compiègne, who lived from ca. 1050 to

1125, along with one of his most prominent students, Peter Abelard (1079–1142). He was also a poet and musician and is one half of the famous doomed love story of Heloise and Abelard.

Quotable Voices

"The key to wisdom is this—constant and frequent questioning, for by doubting we are led to question, and by questioning we arrive at the truth." —Peter Abelard

Abelard is regarded as the dominant philosopher of the twelfth century, as well as the greatest logician of his era. He advocated for using reason in all thoughts and actions, especially and most notably in matters of faith. He's regarded as the first theologian (someone who uses academic principles and rigorous criteria to analyze religious doctrines, texts, and other matters of faith). For example, Abelard held that Christianity-fueled morality had at its center a place of radical intentionalism (the agent's intention, and that alone, determines the moral worth of an action). He was anti-consequence because of a concept he called "moral luck." An example he used to illustrate this concept involved two rich men who each intend to build a poorhouse. But one rich man is robbed, and only the other rich man opens his shelter. To say there is a moral difference between the two men is "insanity," Abelard declared. The deeds themselves, Abelard held, were devoid and neutral in terms of morality. But the agent was subject to evaluation, and the only possible way to do that was to look at their intentions. Thus, they were both morally correct, even though only one followed through with the plan; the robbed man was "lucky" in that he didn't have to do the actual work of building the poorhouse, but he still got credit for being a decent man.

VOLTAIRE AND HEDONISM

Do It Because It Feels Good

One of the most famous and notable writers, playwrights, and humorists in the French language, Voltaire (1694–1778) is the pen name of the writer, historian, and philosopher François-Marie Arouet. Voltaire pioneered a unique ethical and moral philosophy called hedonism. This work represents just one of his many contributions to the great leap forward in philosophical, political, and personal thinking in the eighteenth century known as the Enlightenment.

Voltaire held that humans were not simply determined machines imbued with free will to make the decisions that build their lives. Voltaire believed that while we have will, we are also subject to unassailable natural laws. His ethics called for correct action in a self that had a natural understanding of reason. This meant that those who could understand their ability to reason could be trusted to find the proper course of action themselves. But not all humans were capable of this, and Voltaire held that those who weren't quite smart enough to govern themselves according to the ethical laws of nature needed a moral groundwork laid out for them. This guidance would keep them in line and directed in a moral way. This, Voltaire believed, is what religions were for. (This observation was how Voltaire kept his radical ideas of individual autonomy in check—it was not a good idea to upset the Catholic Church in 1700s Europe.)

LIVING WELL IN EVERY WAY

Voltaire believed that there are certain ways that natural science governs the way we behave. He held that there were certain inalienable truths about human existence with regard to morality. While some philosophers say that the ability to reason and make moral choices out of a framework that was either natural or man-made is one of the things that makes us intrinsically human, Voltaire thought that this was just one element of the human package. He believed in individual liberty. He believed in the full gamut of humanity, which meant, well, living: living it up, living well, and living life to the fullest. He was a hedonist, which is a belief in the seeking of pleasure above all else, and that to do so is the moral imperative. (He wrote erotic poetry, after all, and was a libertine, believing in sexual liberty, a notion that is still somewhat controversial.)

In short, and this was a big part of the Enlightenment, Voltaire advocated personal freedom in almost every way. That included personal freedom, religious freedom, civil liberties, and sexual freedom. These were human truths to him—that humans are free and it is morally their duty to act as such and not to prevent others from acting as such. Put another way, if humanity is not predetermined, then free will must exist; and since we have freedom, we must exercise it in the best way possible.

This meant Voltaire believed in the seeking of personal pleasure, including bodily pleasure, with an ethics rooted in maximizing pleasure and minimizing pain. But unlike the "if it feels good, do it" ethos of the twentieth century and beyond, Voltaire believed that there were actually religious motives at play. If there were divine beings out there, then surely they wanted us to be happy and enjoy the world that was created for us. Thus, the way to be moral is to live a hedonistic lifestyle, as that is what would please God. Ethics, then, are about pleasure and it is moral to seek out pleasure. These ideas were, of course, very contradictory to the moral notions at the time, of which celibacy, restraint, and order were the prevailing theories.

QUESTION EVERYTHING

Another main philosophical component of Voltaire's arguments was Skepticism. In a more specific philosophical frame than just the general idea of Skepticism, he thought Skepticism defended his libertinism. As far as Voltaire was concerned, nothing was immune to questioning, for it was good to question not only monarchies and those in power, but religious systems, for those things affect our happiness and increase our pain. He wasn't against organized religion or Christianity, he just thought that human systems tended to corrupt these institutions.

Quotable Voices

One of Voltaire's most famous quotations is "If God did not exist, if would be necessary to invent him." This has been often misinterpreted. This quote is not Voltaire questioning the existence of God, and if the idea of divinity is a human construct. Actually, Voltaire used the existence of higher beings to justify hedonism as an ethical norm. The quote is really a subtle attack on organized religion, which to Voltaire sets up rules and structures to get between divinity's plan for humanity to enjoy itself and humanity's ability to enjoy itself.

Advocating liberty, pleasure, and freedom in all walks of life was incredibly revolutionary. Voltaire applied his ideas not to just philosophical and personal matters but to political matters as well—which were really just an extension of the personal to the public and to the masses. He openly criticized the Catholic Church and the French government and wrote in support of social reforms, religious reforms, and did so in his writings despite harsh censorship laws in place at the time. Voltaire's ideas and ideals were a major influence on the growing field of political science (particularly John Locke and Thomas Hobbes), and his works definitely led to the movements that brought revolution in both France and America.

JOHN LOCKE AND THE JUST GOVERNMENT

Civil Societies and Social Contracts

John Locke (1632–1704) is one of the most important English philosophers. His thoughts on moral philosophy take a bit from several disciplines, including political science, biology, wider philosophy, and education. Like the many other great minds who helped define the Enlightenment, John Locke advocated a scientific approach and dedication to reason in all inquiries, even ethics, which spanned both the individual and political realms.

The Enlightenment (1685–1815) got underway in Western Europe right around the time of a major political development in Locke's home country of England, one that would inspire a lot of his writings and philosophical ideas. In a 1688 event called the Glorious Revolution, King James II of England was overthrown by a coalition from Parliament, which installed in his place William of Orange, a Dutch royal. Although still a sovereign ruler, William supported the Bill of Rights of 1689, which forever ended the absolute power of the British monarchy in favor of oversight in political decisions from Parliament. This laid the groundwork for the development of formal democracies, as well as the informal notion of giving power to "regular" people, or at least people other than monarchs.

MAKING A CONTRACT

Locke wrote extensively on the idea of a more open form of government. But in the absence of an absolute monarch, there threatened to be a power vacuum or exploitable chaos in which rulers could very well make a grab at power, monarch-style. Something had to be done, and Locke explored the idea of a "social contract." Because there is a lack of a sovereign as the be-all and end-all, then any democratic society, Locke theorized, must have some kind of agreement between the government and the governed. The government is established to maintain agreements and maintain a just society via a system of laws, but underlying that is a social contract, which is an informal agreement or framework that helps determine what is right and wrong within a society. This is then the model by which a culture or society sets its ethical standards and the norms for which positive and negative behavior are recognized and defined on both the individual and political levels. Because it is built on mutual trust and responsibility, a social contract is only as good as those who uphold their part of the agreement. That means a government must rule justly and the people must do their part to uphold the society's values.

Quotable Voices

"[A]ll mankind…being all equal and independent, no one ought to harm another in his life, health, liberty, or possessions." —John Locke

Locke considered there to be a slight wedge between the leaders and the people they lead; Locke calls the populace or the electorate the "civil society." Locke held that an ethical leader—be it a king, president, prime minister, and so on—got his right and approval to lead on loan. A leader was *not* absolute. This means that if a government official in a position of power does not behave according to the prevailing ethical standards (or, say, acts obscenely in his own interests instead of that of the people), a civil society can, should, and will take that power back and replace that person with somebody who does uphold those standards. This system stands in the US, for example; a presidential election is held every four years. It serves as a referendum on the performance and representative abilities of the incumbent president (or if the president's constitutionally limited two terms are up, on the president's political party).

THE IMPORTANCE OF EDUCATION

In 1684 a friend asked Locke—a good person to ask—for his advice on how to properly educate children. Locke thought about it for a long time, and in 1693 published *Some Thoughts Concerning Education*. In the treatise, he carefully lays out links between what he thinks is proper education early in childhood and lasting happiness in adulthood. Foremost, Locke says that happiness requires a healthy body as well as a healthy mind. It's important, then, to instill good healthy habits in kids. In fact, it is a healthy body that allows for the healthiest of thought and readiness for education; the body must be able to do the brain's work. To Locke, physical health was as much of an ethical virtue as intellectual curiosity.

Next, he says that children have to be taught early on how to go after the right things that will bring them happiness. It's important to Locke that this training start early, because children (as well as adults) can be distracted by the world's many attractive frivolities. This is but a first step on Locke's most ethical, virtue-building, happiness-seeking path in which an individual must "deny himself his own desires, cross his own inclinations, and purely follow what reason directs as best, though the appetite lean the other way." This suggests that Locke thought pleasure seeking was natural, but that some of it must be ignored. He divided these lures into "natural wants" and "wants of fancy." Natural wants are just that—natural. They're the ones that we're going to go after and it's perfectly fine, ones that are or seem to be biological. The wants of fancy, though, are false, hollow, man-made desires. It's ethically imperative, Locke writes, for parents and teachers to show children the difference between the two.

LORD SHAFTESBURY AND MORAL SENSE THEORY

The Aesthetics of Ethics

Lord Shaftesbury (1671–1713) was an aristocrat whose real name was Anthony Ashley-Cooper. Shaftesbury made many contributions to Western letters in the late seventeenth and early eighteenth centuries. He was a prominent art theorist and philosopher, trying to define beauty and its powers in both disciplines. But as far as ethics is concerned, his major development is as the father of modern-day moral sense theory.

The first stab at moral sense theory long predates Lord Shaftesbury. The ancient Chinese philosopher Mencius (ca. 372–290 B.C.) was technically the first philosopher to theorize that all human beings are born with a moral sense of right and wrong—a conscious—that becomes more sophisticated over time. Moral sense is also a prominent tenet of most sects of Confucianism, as it is a propelling force in ethical choices. But it was Shaftesbury who really explored the interplay between morality, beauty, and innate understanding. He didn't think he was doing anything particularly new. Working from a neoclassicist point of view, he took two old ideas and fused them: ethics and aesthetics, or the study of the beautiful and artful.

In works such as *An Inquiry Concerning Virtue or Merit* (published without the author's permission in 1699), Shaftesbury equated the way emotions can sniff out the morality of a situation the same way the five physical senses collect information about the world. In other words, Shaftesbury argues that morality can be read with emotional facilities (or moral sense) the same way that an object can be explored through sight, sound, taste, touch, and smell. He also asserts that this moral sense is not something we really learn over time, but rather it is an innate ability by which we learn to use over time, interpreting feelings and experiences through life, forming a sophisticated sense of what is right and wrong.

BEAUTY AND MORALITY

The connection between the physical and moral realms, to Shaftesbury, is the notion of beauty. While beauty is certainly a subjective notion, humans have the ability to recognize, feel, and understand what they individually perceive to be beauty in certain faces, in art, in the natural world, in music, and in food. Our senses may take in all of the physical characteristics, and thus indicators, of beauty, but those senses aren't interpreters of value. Our senses are merely observers of the state of things. To make an evaluation, we need a "sixth sense" to indicate beauty to us so that we can make the leap from information gathering to interpretation. This is an *aesthetic sense*. It is something that must be developed—and according to Shaftesbury, not everyone has this ability innately, even if they have all of the other five senses intact. (He implies the old phrase "there's no accounting for taste.")

It's this aesthetic sense that is the gateway to understanding what is good or bad, or morally right or wrong. The aesthetic sense tells us what we perceive or *know* to be beautiful—which is an innate goodness or specialness. So, too, can that sense be used to determine what is moral simply by paying attention to how it makes a person *feel*. In this regard, moral sense theory is something of a consequentialist theory, because the result of an action, and not the intent or theory behind the action, is what can ultimately be used to label an action "moral" or "immoral."

Quotable Voices

According to Lord Shaftesbury, good morals, or rather moral beauty, is "beauty of the sentiments, the grace of actions, the turn of characters, and the proportions of a human mind." In other words, beauty and ethical goodness are actually the same thing.

This process of observation-feeling-reaction can be used to determine a series of conditions that can be applied to any act to determine if it is moral or not. This means there are, under this theory, universal moral "goods" and "bads" simply because of the reactions they inspire. This determination starts by using the five senses. If you were to see someone being beaten up on the street, for example, you would at least see and hear the attack with your sensory perception abilities. If you had a cultivated aesthetic sense, you would then quickly feel and understand that the attack is quite the opposite of beautiful—that in fact it's quite ugly and repulsive. Your cultivated moral sense would then tell you, completing the equation, that because of all the negative feelings it imparts on you, what you are witnessing in a physical sense is an act of immorality. The best ethical decisions, Shaftesbury reasoned, were the ones full of the most beauty and taste; and positive moral decisions are little works of living art.

CRITICISMS OF
MORAL SENSE THEORY

The philosophical school known as ethical intuitionism has some problems with moral sense theory. Proponents of ethical intuitionism argue that there's something of an intellectual gap and a leap from what are objective observations about natural facts and any interpretive evaluations based on that information. They believe that while a person with a well-cultivated moral sense can observe innate natural properties and use them to make a moral judgment, the morality is neither self-evident nor logically "true" outside of an individual's judgment of it as such. They say that morality isn't self-evident, but that morality isn't as observable as physical properties, particularly to someone with no moral sense. The way those kinds of people can discover the morality of an action is via other ethical inquiries, or if somebody with a better moral sense guides them. In this regard, only those people with that moral sense—which again, isn't everybody—can determine what is or is not moral.

THE PHILOSOPHIES OF BARUCH SPINOZA

Where Divinity and Nature Collide

Baruch Spinoza (1632–1677) was a Dutch-born philosopher from a prominent Jewish family from Portugal. Subscribing to rationalist theories like other major philosophers during the age of reason (a fruitful, post-Renaissance period in the seventeenth century of European philosophical inquiry), Spinoza took the concepts of reason and rationality (as well as some elements of his religious faith) and applied them to moral philosophy. His thoughts were controversial at the time, due to his early moral relativist views that countered mainstream religious thought—so much so that his master work, *Ethics*, was published posthumously in 1677 to little initial acclaim.

Spinoza was an enlightened modernist, and with that came a type of moral relativism. To Spinoza there were no absolute moral truths (or codified belief systems, or innately ethical or unethical actions) because that's just not how the universe was conceived nor how it operated. Relativist positions like this are to be expected from Spinoza, who had a very new idea of the nature of God: he felt that nature and God were one and the same, both constituents of the mystical, directive forces that make the universe run.

When he first began to study philosophy, Spinoza took for fact dualism, a principle established by the French philosopher René Descartes (1596–1650), which held that body and mind were two separate entities. But in *Ethics*, Spinoza wrote that body and mind were two parts of the same whole...a much, much bigger whole. Descartes's notion was that the underlying force of the universe was

God, which led to nature. Spinoza saw God and nature as the same essential substance that made up the reality of existence. In fact, everything spun out from that one central force, Spinoza asserted. He called all living things and objects "modes" of that pure form.

His notion of God was equally controversial and not aligned with regular religious teachings of the time. Spinoza's God was not an almighty figure dictating the lives of humans and other living things, but merely part of an intertwined system, along with nature, that rules with conscious care. God does not control nature, Spinoza attested, because God is nature.

CHOOSE TO NOT CHOOSE

Because of this intricate framework, Spinoza didn't think free will or even spontaneous choice were possible. We merely have the illusion of both. All human behavior is predetermined, Spinoza said, and any notion of freedom exists only in an individual's capacity to understand and know that his or her actions are all predetermined. But in Spinoza's system, humans are not exactly slaves to fate. Rather, he recommended that humanity seek happiness by reaching for the "highest good," which was knowledge and the understanding of God/nature. Truly knowing how things worked was how Spinoza thought humans could be free of fear, escape the pursuit of hollow passions, and overcome other negative concepts. Once they were free, they could have stronger and more positive emotions, and find happiness and contentment.

Another controversial idea of Spinoza's was that because things were predetermined, and because all things stemmed from that which was pure and divine, no being or their actions could be deemed morally "good" or "bad." (The only way that would be a fair assessment is by the individual, in the course of his or her life, as an interpretation of an action, which doesn't really matter because everything is, again, predetermined and quasi-divine.) Spinoza felt that in a world run by the order that God/nature provides, terms like "good" and "evil" were ultimately meaningless. Reality itself is perfection, and if it seems like anything less than that, it's merely due to an individual's inability to full grasp the nature of reality.

About Spinoza

Spinoza was raised in a traditional Jewish upbringing, and his studies consisted mainly of religious texts: the Torah, and works by prophets and rabbis. He was allowed to have a more formal education as a teenager, but when he was seventeen, his father died in battle, and so the younger Spinoza had to drop out of school to take over the family's lucrative importing business. Very quickly, however, he left the business in the control of his brother so he could study philosophy full time. Which he did, in addition to working as an optical lens grinder to pay the bills. He died in 1677 at age forty-four due to a lung illness, likely related to breathing in glass dust all day.

Chapter 9

CLASSIC ETHICS EXERCISES

Studying ethics is important. As a branch of philosophy, ethics helps us unlock key notions of what it means to be human. It also helps us learn how to be good citizens of the world and good individuals, regardless of which philosophical schools or theories we believe to be the most truthful. Knowledge is powerful, and it's certainly good to obtain as much of it as possible. The acquisition of knowledge in the search for truth is as essential as the concept of ethics itself.

This chapter looks at how specific ethical principles can be applied to general living, as well as in thinking out ethical dilemmas. Many notable moral philosophers discussed in this book have used these exercises and others like them to explore, reason their way through, or "prove" their notions about the true nature of ethics. Now it's your turn to give it a try.

THE TROLLEY DILEMMA

Does Somebody Have to Die?

This classic ethics exercise examines, and quite harshly, Kant's Formula of the Universal Law of Nature. Basically, in theory, Kant's idea that a good personal philosophy is one that an individual wouldn't mind making a universal maxim...but is it a really sound moral philosophy if there's a body count?

Philippa Foot

Foot is best known for this ethical game, which has appeared in hundreds of periodicals, brain teaser books, and texts over the past few decades. One of her other major breakthroughs was an exploration of the foundational virtues of morality and ethics. Specifically, Foot considered wisdom, courage, and temperance to be the most virtuous of the virtues.

The "trolley dilemma" is an ethical test scenario (hypothetically, thankfully) devised in the 1960s by British moral philosopher Philippa Foot and expanded upon by American philosopher Judith Jarvis Thomson in the 1980s. Both Foot and Thomson sought to create a very tense moment that required immediate action and left no room for a lengthy philosophy discussion or a lengthy reasoning process. In other words, it's applied ethics when it matters most, and urgently at that. Thomson pinpointed several different reactions to the trolley dilemma, each one correlating to a different major ethical school of thought: utilitarianism, deontology, divine command theory, ethical relativism, and virtue ethics.

ONE PROBLEM, MANY "SOLUTIONS"

Imagine that you are the driver of a trolley. It goes around a bend, and you see five people working hard on the track, repairing it. Immediately after spotting them, the track dips down into a valley out of sight of the workers, sending your trolley down too. Once the trolley comes up again out of the valley, it will almost immediately strike and definitely kill those track workers. However, as the trolley ascends out of the valley, you spot a track leading off to the right. But there is one man at work on that track. There isn't time for the five men on track A or the one man on track B to jump off and get to safety, so it's entirely up to you, the trolley driver, to decide what to do.

So, what do you do? Do you stay on the track you're on and definitely kill five men, or do you throw a switch, and move over to the new track where you'll definitely kill one man?

Option #1: Throw the switch and move to the new track.

You believe that you are maximizing the well-being of others—given the options, it's better for five people to survive at the expense of one life.

Analysis: Choosing this option is what a utilitarian would do. As they value the consequence over the action itself, they believe the most morally superior action is the one that leads to the greatest good for the most people. From a utilitarian perspective, saving five lives is the best possible outcome.

Option #2: Throw the switch and move to the new track.

You believe that virtue is of the utmost importance, and as a virtuous person, saving five lives is charitable and compassionate—at least more charitable and compassionate than saving just one life.

Analysis: This is the choice and reasoning of a virtue ethicist. Those who adhere to this theory determine the morality of an action via a consideration of character and virtues—good intent means more than the action or the consequences. The consequence here is that one man will die, but it's still a virtuous act because the trolley driver's heart was in the right place when making the decision.

Option #3: Don't throw the switch. Stay on the track. Strike and definitely kill the five workers.

Analysis: This is the correct course of action for a deontologist, or Kantian. This approach is all about the innate morality or immorality (or rightness and wrongness) of the actions. It's a bit of an ethical loophole, but in deontological thinking, the act of staying on the track and killing five men is more ethical than killing one. Why? Because to switch to the other track would be a conscious choice—and one that would end in killing. And killing is wrong. (Similarly, under divine command theory, it would also be wrong to switch over. Divine command theorists align their actions with God's will—and God has decided that these five men are going to die on this track, via this trolley.)

Quotable Voices

"You ask a philosopher a question and after he or she has talked for a bit, you don't understand the question any more." —Philippa Foot

Option #4: Don't throw the switch. That man on the other track would die, and you would be complicit in his death, which would be both culturally unacceptable and illegal.

Analysis: This stance is a demonstration of ethical relativism. In other words, there is no good choice for the trolley driver because someone is going to die. The thing that causes the trolley driver to act, or rather not act and stay the course, is that actively killing is wrong and against the law in the trolley driver's culture. The driver would be technically guilty of murder (or manslaughter), whereas in the killing of five people, it's merely an accident.

THE PRISONER'S DILEMMA

Just Confess (Or Maybe Don't)

Here's another exercise for applying some moral philosophy concepts. It's called the "prisoner's dilemma," and it was developed in the 1950s not by ethicists but by mathematicians Merrill Flood, Melvin Dresher, and Albert Tucker at the famous and powerful RAND Corporation.

The RAND Corporation's Role in This Ethical Exercise

Not only are ethics intrinsically involved in this dilemma, but so are math and probability. RAND was tasked with trying to predict how various nuclear stand-off scenarios could resolve, based on game theory. The prisoner's dilemma helped sort out all the ways a potentially deadly Cold War showdown might go, based on who acted first and who backed down, and so on.

Here's the scenario: Two members of a criminal gang, Tommy and Frank, have been arrested for robbing a bank. The police and prosecutors are certain that Tommy and Frank robbed the bank (hence their arrests), but they lack enough evidence to convict both of them on the main charge. Wanting to send them each to prison for a year or so on a lesser charge, prosecutors offer both Tommy and Frank some deals. This leaves Tommy and Frank with two essential choices:

ETHICS 101

- Option #1: Betray their compatriot, and pin the crime entirely on the other guy.
- Option #2: Continue to be silent, admit to nothing, and not sell the other one out.

DECISIONS, DECISIONS

What is the best choice? It depends on the possible outcome, and there are a lot more than two outcomes:

- If Tommy and Frank both finger the other one, they'll both serve two years in prison.
- If Tommy rats out Frank, but Frank stays silent, Tommy goes free. Frank serves three years in prison on the main charge.
- Similarly, if Frank rats out Tommy, but Tommy stays silent, it's Frank who goes free and Tommy is left to serve the full three years for the robbery.
- If neither man confesses nor pins the blame on the other guy, they'll both serve a year in prison (and on the lesser charge).

WHEN HONESTY ISN'T THE BEST POLICY

A few caveats are needed to eliminate any other influencing factors: There is no other reward or punishment for Tommy or Frank, as they'll serve their time in separate prisons, if need be. Nor can they collude to find the best option for all involved. Both Tommy and

Frank are being held separately in solitary confinement and they have no way to communicate with the outside world, or with each other. So, what should they do?

They betray each other. A rational prisoner with his self-interest in mind would betray the other person. And since both are rational human beings, and neither man wants to go to jail, each would consider only his own well-being and happiness because the consequences of considering otherwise (like jail) are not good.

But it's an ethical quandary. Both men pursuing the individual reward leads both prisoners to betrayal, but if both stay silent they'd each get a better reward (on the whole). However, if both confess, the outcome for each man would be worse than if they had both remained silent.

The Prisoner's Dilemma in Sports

Is taking steroids in sports ethical? That's a big question, with many thoughts on the matter on both sides and in between, but it's an especially interesting conundrum with regard to the mentioned prisoner's dilemma. Performance-enhancing drugs increase an athlete's abilities, but using those drugs causes some potentially dangerous side effects. All pro athletes of a given sport have relatively similar skill levels, and the drugs work generally the same on each of those athletes. It's to all of the athletes' advantages if nobody takes those drugs—because if everybody used them, then no one athlete would have an edge, and all the athletes would be subject to the side effects of taking the drugs. But if just one or two athletes take the drugs, then those athletes would gain an advantage, but the disadvantageous side effects would become a problem for them.

EUBULIDES OF MILETUS AND THE SORITES PARADOX

A Heap of Trouble

Eubulides of Miletus was a fourth-century B.C. Greek thinker. Unlike most of the other Greek figures noted in this book, Eubulides wasn't a philosopher or religious leader. Rather, he was a logician—the guy who kept the philosophers on their toes by making them aware of logical flaws in their arguments, or at least he made them think things through a bit more so their reasoning could be justified with a logical, rational argument. Eubulides is best known for a series of puzzles, which are essentially ethically loaded brain teasers. The one of interest here is known as the "sorites paradox."

The sorites paradox is a philosophical problem with no real solution. It exposes the natural fallacies in logic and reason that can occur in the discussion of a vast, nonscientific or nonempirical discipline such as philosophy or ethics. If anything, it's a parable to demonstrate the limitations of language, and how one must be careful in choosing one's words, because words (and the ethical concepts they describe) can wind up sounding arbitrary, or mean different things to different people. And if words are arbitrary and subjective, well, then the truths they describe just might be arbitrary or subjective too, which isn't a good thing in the universal truth-seeking mission of moral philosophers.

Sorites is from the Greek word *soros*, which means "heap." In ancient Greece, when the sorties paradox was developed by Eubulides of Miletus, it was called *soros*. As the Greek term suggests, this is a rhetorical puzzle about the nature of a heap. How would one describe a heap? How many, say, grains of wheat, make up a heap? Is one grain of wheat a heap? No, of course not. How about two? Three? You have to say something is a "heap" at some point—but where is that point? Eubulides said you could declare a heap at grain one or two...when it's decidedly not a heap. Is, then, a heap a matter of "I know it when I see it"? It could be, but that answer is not a good use of those ethical truth-seeking tools of rationalistic thought.

Quotable Voices

Contemporary New York University philosophy professor Peter Unger has applied the sorites paradox to the difference between human beings: "Can a single cell here mean the difference between me and no me? That's almost an affront to my dignity!"

"I know it when I see it" is a creeping, recurring theme in ethics. Relying on the notion that language is subjective, and that thoughts and feelings are individualistic and unique, is an admission to the idea that certain themes cannot be defined universally. And, problematically, these are the big themes. No two people, for example, could possibly both give the same definition of happiness. Like sensing when a pile is a heap, happiness is a feeling that cannot be precisely defined. And that's problematic to the study of ethics, because happiness is the end goal for many major theorists.

COMMUNICATION ISSUES

The *falakros* or "the bald man" is a variation on the original sorites paradox, only that the material in question is in the negative, and increasingly so. The bald man describes a characteristic to prove the point of how hard it is to define something. Would you describe a man with only one hair on his head to be bald? Sure, it's only one hair. (Even though he isn't technically bald.) How about two? How about...10,000? If at 10,000 you would say no, that that man isn't bald, well then, once more, where is the limit?

THE SPIDER IN THE URINAL

An Ethical Quandary

As part of his 1986 essay "Birth, Death, and the Meaning of Life," New York University professor and philosopher Thomas Nagel presented a true-story-meets-ethical-dilemma that came to be nicknamed "The Spider in the Urinal." The fable-like, troubling story brings up many ethical issues, such as the morality of interference and if it is in fact ethical to interject one's own actions into another's life in the name of the pursuit of happiness...especially if the agent is not able to tell or know if his or her action will lead to increased happiness on the part of the recipient.

Nagel used the same restroom every day while teaching at Princeton, and every day he encountered the same spider, living out his days in a urinal. He "didn't seem to like it," Nagel wrote of the spider. Neither did Nagel, and so he set out to act on behalf of the spider. His intentions and motivations were noble—he recognized what appeared, from his point of view, the spider was suffering from. But his intentions and motivations came from a place of his own mind-set, based on his experiences and virtues. He acted from a place of moral goodness, with the intent to help another living being and increase happiness and lessen suffering. And yet, Nagel didn't consider the consequences, or at least he presumed that the consequence would be all positive, and that the spider would be better off because of his actions. (This exposes a flaw in consequentialism.)

"[I]t might be his natural habitat, but because he was trapped by the smooth porcelain overhang, there was no way for him to get out even if he wanted to, and no way to tell whether he wanted to....So, one day toward the end of the term I took a paper towel from the wall dispenser and extended it to him. His legs grasped the end of the towel and I lifted him out and deposited him on the tile floor."

The next day Nagel returned and found the spider dead on the floor, where it remained for a week until the cleaning crew came through, and it was swept up.

CREATURE DISCOMFORTS

Was Nagel's unsolicited offer of help morally acceptable? Or was it immoral of Nagel to interfere with the life and happiness pursuit of another being, simply because he judged the spider's life to be inadequate? Oddly enough, it's only after the fact that an analysis of the spider's quality of life can even be possible. In retrospect, and after "good-natured" interference by another came into play, it was clear that the spider was having a fine time hanging out in a urinal of a men's restroom all day. This was what the spider wanted to do, and one could argue that it was morally wrong for Nagel to interfere.

On the other hand the spider is a nonrational being. It is not capable of advanced reasoning or logic, which is to say it cannot make decisions about its own happiness. (The fact that a spider may not even have a concept of happiness, due to its lack of ability to reason, is another ethical quandary unto itself.)

Is it immoral to interfere in the life of a nonrational being, such as a spider? One could argue that Nagel's action was immoral, because Nagel had no right to change the trajectory of another living being's life. One could also argue that Nagel's action was moral, because he acted from the virtue of wanting to help improve the spider's life by removing it from the trap of a urinal. Nagel could even be said to have had an obligation to help that spider, because he saw an injustice and it is his moral duty, as a human being with advanced rationality and inner virtues, to help.

Nagel and Animal Ethics

Nagel had often written about the nature—and possible fallacies—of consciousness. One of his most famous works is a 1974 essay called "What Is It Like to Be a Bat?" In it he argued that all organisms, including animals, have some sort of specific awareness. As the title suggests, Nagel set forth the notion that bats, for example, have an innate understanding of what it feels like to be a bat.

His intention played a part in his action, as did the underlying virtue that caused him to act. But the act itself led to bad consequences. So, depending on your ethical point of view, or if you think actions or intent is where the heart of morality lies, the argument could go either way. At any rate, this was not a moral act under the heading of consequentialism, because the ends did not justify the means. But a virtue ethicist or deontologist would say that Nagel is in the clear, and he should be proud of his actions, because his act was born out of a desire to help and moral fortitude.

THE COW IN THE FIELD PROBLEM

Knowing What You Know

Any discussion of ethical principles—or of philosophy in general, for that matter—comes from a place of knowledge. In philosophy this is a field called epistemology, which is the study of the nature of knowledge. To engage in such a study, all parties must start from a mutual, understood place before any discussion of our greater drives or obligations can take place. In other words, the parties must have a shared knowledge. But this is philosophy, the fine art of questioning everything. So really, how can we be sure that what we know is real, and that is perceived the same way by another, or if it's even proven to be true at all? According to the creator of the "cow in the field" problem, twentieth-century philosopher and epistemologist Edmund Gettier, there's a danger in the notion of knowledge. Knowledge is commonly defined as a belief that can be justified and proven as true (justified belief is true knowledge), but this is not always the case. *Everything*, even cold hard truths, can't really be trusted.

The cow in the field problem, also called the Gettier problem, goes like this: A farmer owns a prized cow. But he hasn't seen it a while, and he fears that it's wandered off. But a visitor, a mailman, comes to the farm. Upon hearing about the farmer's problem, the mailman tells the farmer not to worry, because he's seen the cow in a nearby pasture. The farmer is relieved and is almost entirely certain that the mailman is correct—after all, the mailman has no reason to lie. Moreover, the mailman would be easily caught in the lie if he were lying, and a nearby field is a logical place for a lost cow to turn up.

So the mailman leaves and the farmer goes to this nearby pasture to find the cow. Sure enough, he sees the familiar black-and-white, cow-shaped thing. Satisfied, he goes about his day and waits for the cow to wander back home. Later on, the mailman returns to check up on the missing cow. The cow is there, but it is now standing in a small grove of trees. It's possible the cow moved to the wooded area after having been spotted in the pasture by both the mailman and the farmer...except that hanging from a tree in the middle of the pasture is a large sheet of black-and-white paper. Clearly, the farmer and the mailman both mistook that object for the missing cow.

WHAT'S THE PROBLEM?

The conundrum is this: Even though the cow *was* in the pasture (or at least nearby, or at least it had been in the pasture), was the farmer "correct" when he "knew" it was there? The farmer's conclusion was correct: He thought, or rather "knew," that the cow was in the pasture, and the cow indeed was in the pasture. However, the reasoning he used to get to the correct solution was incorrect. He visualized the cow, mistaking some hanging paper for his animal. This means that there are actually two different and separate notions of "correct." One correct notion is in the mind, and that notion can only be specific and individual to the observer, or agent. The other notion occurs completely outside of the mind, and that notion is determined in part by a second observer, in relation to the first.

In other words, the truth and the truth as it is *perceived* might be two different things, even if they align. The farmer's belief in what he thought was the truth was not justified, and he would have been wrong had the cow not actually been nearby, which is unrelated to the reasoning at hand. He was accidentally correct. This means his justified true belief was not justified, nor true, and is thus not knowledge.

On Edmund Gettier (1927–)

The cow in the field problem was a part of "Is Justified True Belief Knowledge?" a three-page paper Gettier published in 1963. The philosophy professor thought so little of the essay that he didn't even bother submitting it to American or English-language academic journals. He had a friend translate it into Spanish, and it was published in South America. Later available in English, it became one of the most famous and important works of philosophy and logic of the twentieth century.

The ramifications not only affect philosophy and ethics, but they have an impact on most any decision that humans make. As the cow in the field problem illustrates, the justification that leads us to make reasonable, rational, and even ethical decisions could be either circumstantial or even circumspect.

THE LIAR PARADOX

When the Truth Is False

In another paradoxical exercise in which to explore the fallacies of human communication, Eubulides of Miletus presented "the liar" paradox. It's usually presented like this: A man says, "This sentence is false. I am lying." So, is what he says true or false?

This question can be debated for a long time with neither side coming around. There are legitimate, reasonable arguments for both sides. And both sides can use clear, direct, and rational thought, rather than feeling, to arrive at their conclusions.

For example, you could say it is virtuous to believe that another human (or all humans) is innately good and acts in his or her self-interest, which is also the divine sense of doing good. So, you could say he's telling the truth overall. Or you could say that the human acts in his or her own self-interest, which can be quite nasty and self-serving. Could you therefore say the man is lying overall? Quite the paradox.

Let's break this down. A man says that he's lying. So, is he lying about lying? If he is telling the truth, he's lying. This means he's not telling the truth. About lying. And around it goes in circles. It's like the saying, "Which came first, the chicken or the egg?" but with philosophical ramifications. How you choose to answer also gives you an idea of what ethical school you might fall under. (Not answering at all means you might be an existentialist or a nominalist.)

The paradox arrives at a contradiction through the act of reasoning. Circular logic then upends itself. What is true? What is false? Is a true statement about truth a lie? This riddle has been around for more than 2,000 years, and there's still no clear consensus by ethicists on what the "true" answer may be. That's because, well, it's a paradox. It can be proven to be both true and false via its own reasoning.

If anything is proven by this paradox, it's that there can be flaws in logic. Logic is, at its core, a process, that if followed to the letter may not wind up providing a truthful answer. Even though logic and reasoning are supposed to lead thinkers to an objective truth, that may not always happen, depending on the complexity and nuance of the circumstance. This means any sort of ethical truth that results from a logical process may not be truthful if the source material is less than truthful (or, at the very least, contradictory).

Another Liar's Paradox

In the sixth century B.C., the Greek philosopher Epimenides came up with a thought experiment very similar to the liar paradox. He wrote: "All Cretans are liars…One of their own poets has said so." Epimenides's use of language subtly changes the aim of the problem—it's not about "I" but rather the people of Crete. However, the language is a bit more navigable than that of the liar's paradox. In fact, the Cretan thought experiment is not even a true paradox, because that one poet may know of an honest Cretan, so he could be lying when he says all are liars. The truth of the statement could all boil down to a false statement from one individual.

THE SHIP OF THESEUS PROBLEM

The Question of Identity

The way the Earth rotates on its axis while also revolving around the sun represents two kinds of constant movement or change. But the planet still remains the same thing as it moves through time, from daytime to nighttime and back again, and as the days turn into weeks, and so on into the future. Tectonic plates subtly shift a little, temperatures change, individual lives enter and exit, and entire species both develop and die out. In short, the Earth is in a state of constant flux, but it is never not Earth—it is always still itself.

Similarly, human beings are always growing, changing, and aging, but one of the defining characteristics of being human is a well-developed sense of self, or identity. And yet, every experience happens to the same ever-changing body, to the same mind and soul, with each experience affecting how the next is handled, and so on. There are even layers of our identities, based on how we see ourselves and how we interact with others. Circumstances may change—school, work, relationships, physical ailments, and so on—but we are never not ourselves. You remember childhood because it happened to *you*. You are the same person then as you are now.

But *are* you? Are you really? You're also a completely different person now than you were as a child because of the different experiences you've had and the decisions you've faced. Moreover, biologically and physically you are made up of completely different cells. In fact, the body's cells are constantly dying, and are being replaced and regenerated. It's an oft-cited statistic that every seven years, no cell remains the same. You're a new "you" every seven years or so, cell-wise. And you'll be a new you another seven years from now. You will always be a work in progress.

The "ship of Theseus" is an ancient philosophical thought experiment that seeks to address these kinds of questions. While it may not quite solve them, the problem is an interesting conundrum for students of moral philosophy—in which any aspect of identity involves self-interest, intent, and the very nature of that "personal" place from which moral decisions derive.

IDENTITY CRISIS

Nearly 2,000 years ago, a Greek historian and biographer named Plutarch (ca. A.D. 45–120) popularized a riddle that became known as the ship of Theseus problem (or paradox). In his work called *Life of Theseus*, Plutarch writes of the ship of the mythical Athenian warrior-king Theseus. This ship originally had thirty oars and was made up primarily of planks. It was used by generations of Theseus's successors. Each time a plank became old, rotted, or otherwise destroyed, it would be replaced by a newer, stronger plank. Plutarch directly suggests that this is a metaphor for change and growth. He also brings up the inherent philosophical issue. Over time, Theseus's entire ship had been replaced, here and there, bit by bit, one piece at a time, so that no part of the original ship Theseus first sailed remained. Can one even call this Theseus's ship anymore? Is it the same ship in any way, and if not, when did it stop being the same ship?

While Plutarch solidified and popularized the ship of Theseus problem, philosophers both before and after him weighed the paradox. For example, Greek philosopher Heraclitus (ca. 535–475 B.C.) suggested that the completely revised boat was the same as the original boat because they had both sailed in the same waters. Plutarch dismissed that notion because a river changes more often than even the boat, as a river recedes, separates, and returns (which is to say nothing of the cycle of water, clouds, and rain). English philosopher Thomas Hobbes (1588–1679) added another intriguing element to the puzzle: What if all the original planks had been collected after removal to create a second ship. Would that *also* be the ship of Theseus, or would it be any more or any less so than the slowly replaced ship of Theseus? John Locke had another approach, toying with the idea of *when* the change from "old" to "new" occurs, if it even does change at all. He used the metaphor of a sock with a patched-up hole. Is it still the same sock after the one patch? How about the next? Or the next, until all the original material has been replaced with patches? Locke nearly takes the ship of Theseus into sorites paradox territory.

Variations on a Theme

A similar variant of the ship of Theseus paradox that appears in a lot of philosophical texts is called "grandfather's axe." Instead of a ship consisting of dozens of wood planks, it questions the essence of an old axe if the head has been replaced, and then later, the handle. The story has often been apocryphally cited as being about the axe of both George Washington and Abraham Lincoln.

The great Aristotle weighed in too. He held that "four causes" constitute a thing, and that an analysis of those causes can help solve the ship of Theseus paradox. There's the design (formal cause), the objects of which it's made (material cause), the intended purpose (final cause), and how an object is made (efficient cause). The objects (tools) used to make the new boat parts were the same, as was the purpose and technique of the manufacturing tasks. But because the overall design did not change—the formal cause was most important to Aristotle—the new boat remains a legitimate ship of Theseus.

In the end, it makes us question what makes up a thing. What constitutes its identity? Its spirit or moral center perhaps?

Chapter 10

APPLIED ETHICS

Ethics can only take us so far if we only focus on a bunch of theories about how humans are, or how we ought to act. Ethics don't exist solely as theories and idea; ethics are meant to lead directly to action. Therefore we have applied ethics, or moral philosophy in action and in pratice.

Although the most prominent moral philosophies were hammered out centuries ago, their finer points remain open to question. Ethics don't exist in a vacuum, and they don't stand still. They're systems that contain multitudes of practical rules that can be learned and adapted into any number of real-life situations. Indeed, ethicists have attempted to find the universals of morality that apply to all humans and, it would seem, all walks of life. Ethics are a big part of the decision-making processes in many of today's professions and fields, and are especially relevant as the world faces rapidly changing and as-yet unknown challenges both now and in the future.

This chapter will look at how to apply some of the ethical concepts covered earlier in this book. Ethics, or virtues, are a vital tool in a civilized society, and they apply to nearly every sector of the professional world. The reasons to be ethical are of course complicated, and will be discussed. Is it important to be ethical because it's good for business to be ethical; or is it ethical to be morally correct in business because it's important to be ethical to human beings, period? There are arguments for both positions, and more.

BUSINESS AND PROFESSIONAL ETHICS

Morals on the Job

Business ethics are moral values that a company employs in shaping its strategies and practices, and/or in creating a standard to which it holds its employees. Like an individual, ethics must address big-picture concerns (how it does business) and individual ones (how employees are treated). Determining what actions are or are not moral is tricky for a business—a business is not an individual, but neither is a business a single entity with the power of reason (rather it is at the mercy of the opinions and interests of many), nor is a business a governing body with a moral obligation to its people.

Is there even a place for ethics in the world of business? It depends on what you consider to be the imperative of a business. One could argue that businesses don't need to worry about ethics, because they are not rational beings that must adhere to a moral code—that they exist solely to make money for its owners or shareholders. (Which, in a way, is not unlike the ultimate human goal of "happiness.") From a Machiavellian perspective, businesses should be allowed to do whatever it takes to make money, and as much money, however they can. But they'd have to do that while still operating within the confines of the law. From an ethical perspective, it would be against the self-interest of a business to break the law—or antagonize its employees, or engage in price-gouging, or sell a faulty product—because that would harm the public image of the business. Decreased public trust, not to mention charges of doing harm, leads to decreased revenues, thus hurting its imperative to make money.

A company that operates in an entirely legal way might not do so in ways that are just or even palatable. For example, a business that fires a large number of employees and then reroutes that money to executives isn't behaving illegally, but this action would have an incredibly negative impact on a lot of people and cast the company's decision-makers in a negative light. Even if such practices were perfectly legal, most ethical schools would probably find them to be morally suspect.

The Origin of Business Ethics

The modern business ethics conversation began in the late 1960s as an outgrowth of the social and political activism movements. Issues such as social quality and government accountability came to the forefront of public interest, and more and more people started examining the authority, practices, and motivations of large corporations.

But businesses are a part of society, and an influential one—they're publicly present, and they have a huge impact on the economy by way of selling goods or services, paying employees, paying taxes, and so forth. For these reasons, businesses are not immune to the moral standards that guide individuals or governments. Ultimately, it's in a company's best interest to maintain good relations with the public (and its shareholders, and its customers) by operating from a morally good standpoint.

LABOR ETHICS

Relativism comes into play in a big way with business ethics. For example, it's considered unethical—and illegal, actually—to pay workers in the United States anything less than the minimum wage. (Some would argue for a higher standard, such as a "fair" or "livable" wage, but those standards are harder to define.) Though the minimum wage varies from state to state, it is set at a federal level and no one can be paid less than that minimum on an hourly basis. For this reason, labor costs for manufacturing in the United States are quite high. This is the main reason why many American companies have moved operations overseas. A shoe manufacturer, for example, may choose to operate a factory in the developing world and pay workers pennies to assemble a pair of shoes, whereas that same operation in the US could cost a hundred times that in labor. (There is also far less regulation of factories and working conditions in other nations, both of which cost money and slow down production.) Also potentially problematic is the issue of child labor. In the United States, labor laws prevent children from working in factories, and certainly not for eighteen hours a day, in part because such practices are considered immoral in our culture. Other countries have different standards in regard to child labor.

At the end of the day, businesses operate overseas to maximize profits. But such businesses are actually skirting moral-based US laws. A business engages in exploitation when it pays workers overseas as little as possible simply because it can get away with it. This is all due to moral relativism. One might try to explain away these practices using the tenets of moral relativism. But such arguments fall apart because the relative comparison itself is false: Two different cultures and two different moral blueprints are being compared on a relative basis. That shoe company is exploiting cultural differences in an overseas location to drive down costs and drive up profits—it is not providing low-wage jobs out of respect for the moral standards of another culture.

ADVERTISING ETHICS

There's more moral shaky ground in the areas of advertising and marketing. Advertising "works" on everyone, even the most sophisticated consumer, because messages about products find a way to embed themselves in our brains over time. (If advertising didn't work, it wouldn't be used.) However, ethical concerns accompany that power to manipulate. For example, most reasonably savvy adults understand that advertising claims are exaggerations. Such claims are either stated directly (e.g., "It's the dog food your dog will love best!") or dramatized or suggested (e.g., a dog happily eating the food and then dancing on its hind legs, thanks to the magic of visual special effects). In other words, advertisements lie.

Is it ethical to proclaim falsehoods, even if people know the claims are false and know to take them with a grain of salt? Perhaps not, because some viewers are highly impressionable, children in particular. Toward the end of the twentieth century, the federal government cracked down on advertising to children because many thought their trust and innocence were being exploited. The main purveyors of ads to children at the time were makers of sugar cereals and fast food, products that could be tied to a growing childhood obesity epidemic. Businesses have a responsibility not to harm their clients in the pursuit of making money, and advertising practices can easily cause a company to step over this boundary.

ETHICS IN POLITICS

Leading with Care

Way back when, philosophy started as guidelines for politicians. In ancient Greece (and to major philosophers such as John Locke and Niccolo Machiavelli), philosophy and politics were intertwined. Socrates, Plato, and others frequently wrote about and discussed the best way by which men (only men at the time) could reach down deep and apply the noble virtues they possessed so as to lead others in a just and ethical way. The baseline of personal ethics informed politics, but then personal ethics also became a subject of its own inquiry.

Today, with so much work already done to develop ethics and investigate the meaning of terms like "just" and "ethical," it's incumbent upon politicians to lead in an ethical manner. Politicians chosen by the people (or born into power) face many specific ethical challenges, all ultimately boiling down to a need to rule and govern in ways that are just and fair. But how do they do that, and who do they most serve?

Running for office or holding an elected position brings great power...and great responsibility. A vote for a candidate is an expression of trust, and politicians must try to both represent the voters' interests and keep their own campaign promises to the best of their abilities. And yet politicians by and large do not enjoy a reputation as a group of people who have a great deal of integrity or moral fiber. Every election season, the same displeasures with politicians soak the cultural ether, primarily revolving around negative campaigning, truth-bending or outright lying, and a collective curiosity as to just why someone is interested in pursuing power.

Most politicians have a genuine interest in public service, but many politicians have differing ideas on what that means. Simply defining who "the public" is can be a challenge. Do politicians serve the people? If so, then which people? All the people or just their voters? Do politicians serve an area's interests, and do the needs of the individuals of that area differ from those of the major institutions or employers that also occupy that area? Or is it the responsibility of a politician to serve legal constructs, ideals, or constitutions in an effort just to keep the peace? All of these targets may have conflicting values. Democracy works slowly, and change is hard to come by, so a commitment to change to the morally good requires resolve.

PUBLIC VERSUS PERSONAL LIFE

Another ethical issue with regard to politicians is their personal life. In the US, there are countless examples of elected officials who, when news of their extramarital affairs become public, have to issue a public apology and then resign their position. In other countries, such as France, it's more culturally acceptable for adults, and politicians, to have affairs. Constituents in such countries are able to separate a politician's personal life from his or her public life, and then judge the political performance of their elected officials solely on that basis. It's an ethical quandary to determine if politicians' private lives are indeed private, because they are also public figures. Moreover, opinions of political figures can change if they fail to uphold long-held cultural values—and their performance as public figures can then be called into question.

Money can also certainly cloud the ethical purity of politicians. When campaigns receive money from individuals or organizations who are not also their constituents, a potential conflict of interest is created. Who are well-funded politicians truly beholden to: their donors or their voters?

BEST INTENTIONS

We also wonder about a politician's intentions. There are certainly benefits to the job—being famous and having tremendous power and influence are very attractive to some people. But political jobs bring with them intense scrutiny and criticism. Everything one says, does, or votes on is fair game. It makes a person wonder why anybody would ever want to be a politician. There are lots of reasons, and they come from all over the ethical spectrum. Some politicians have a genuine desire to effect change via legislation, or working from inside the "the belly of the beast." Others might be coming from a place of self-interest—the desire for power, for example. Motivations can be multiple, of course, and some politicians feel compelled by a desire to defeat "evil"—or their opponent, who, if the negative campaign ads are to be believed, would be a very bad choice for voters. But no matter what reasons politicians give on the campaign trail for wanting the job, we can't help but wonder why they're *really* running for office.

POLITICS AND VIRTUES

Despite the persistent cliché that all politicians are corrupt liars, we do on the whole demand and expect our politicians to be trustworthy and truthful. Perhaps this is because we have to—we have to vote for somebody, and we want to believe that the candidate we select is the morally superior one. It's in our self-interest and that of the greater good to elect the candidates who we think are the most virtuous, and to reject the ones who will be easily swayed by money and "special interests." In American democracy, the "checks and balances" innate in the system (along with whistle-blowers, a free press, and an impeachment process) have been set in place to help limit that kind of corruption, and the idea that leaders are above the law.

Quotable Voices

"Men say I am a saint losing himself in politics. The fact is that I am a politician trying my hardest to become a saint." —Mahatma Gandhi

We want, and expect, our politicians to be a little bit better than average. We want them to lead by example and be the best of the best (an image we sometimes force upon them with fervor and hagiography, elevating them to demigod status in a way to justify giving them so much power and trusting they use it wisely). We want them to exhibit virtue ethics and to be the very best. We want them to be truthful and responsible, to truly care, and to work hard to find solutions to the problems we face.

MEDICAL ETHICS

First Do No Harm

Physicians and other medical and healthcare workers famously take the Hippocratic oath. Named for an ancient Greek physician, the oath begins with the simple directive of "First, do no harm." In other words, it steers medical professionals to a place of positive activity—save lives, heal bones, manage illnesses, and alleviate discomfort—and do *not* make things worse. In other words, their job is to preserve life and make aims to improve the quality of life, as reasonably necessary. It's in words like "necessary" and "quality" where problems develop. Ethics in medicine can help professionals navigate the everyday, case-by-case choices in treatment they have at their disposal, particularly in those gray areas between "help" and "harm."

One major issue facing healthcare is the allocation of that healthcare. Resources, in terms of doctors, medicine, hospital space, and more are generally limited, and they are very expensive. Some countries have enacted government-sponsored healthcare, sending the message that it is morally good for all people, regardless of station in life, to have access to healthcare services. In other countries, healthcare is on par with a business, opening up the ethical question of who should get access to those limited resources. Should only those who can afford to pay the price have that access? If so, what is the ethical notion behind this position? Do people have a right to refuse to pay for health insurance as a matter of expressing their integrity and autonomy, and in so doing pass their medical costs on to others, or perhaps even forgo medical services altogether?

ETHICS OF PRESCRIPTION DRUGS

Prescription drugs carry with them their own set of ethical questions. Medications are a multibillion-dollar industry, and they have literally saved countless lives by managing or curing many medical conditions. Making new drugs is an expensive undertaking, but the upside is that a new wonder drug could potentially earn billions for its manufacturer. Take, for example, a hypothetical pill that early tests showed to cure heart disease. It is in the interest of the drug company to get that pill out to the public as quickly as possible, because it can earn the company a lot of money. But it's also in the good of the public interest for the company to maximize its efforts and get it to market quickly so that it can improve the quality of life or even extend life to those who take it.

However, in the United States, a drug must go through rigorous testing by the US Food and Drug Administration (FDA) before it reaches the market. This testing is done to ensure the safety and efficacy of a drug. This is a thorough vetting process that can take as long as ten years. Is it ethical for the FDA to sit so long on a drug that could help people now? Maybe, because even though a given drug could help some people now, it's possible that it could help so many more later after post-testing improvements. Conversely, a drug may at first seem to be safe and effective, but FDA testing reveals it to be anything but safe or not at all effective. The questions run even deeper: Is it ethical for a company to rush a beneficial drug to market (and earn a great profit) even if that drug hasn't been totally proven to be safe or effective? Without that FDA testing, it could be seen as immoral to release such a drug.

LIFE-AND-DEATH ISSUES

Some issues—and questions—that doctors have to deal with involve the "boundaries of life." There are so many different perspectives in the medical community on this issue, and they represent a wide breadth of people. Many doctors are solely scientific-minded, for example, while other doctors have a deeply held moral obligation to help or heal. Speaking very generally, these two types of doctors may hold completely different opinions about abortion, euthanasia, or organ donation. And there's a sliding scale, of course, between those two extremes. The scientific doctor may view abortion as a simple medical procedure where no boundaries of life issues come into play at all. The religious doctor may be extremely opposed to abortion and not perform the procedure under any circumstance. Another doctor may do it only early in the pregnancy and only to save the life of the mother if complications arise. These ethical viewpoints affect how these doctors work, and they also bring up other ethical questions. For example, does a doctor have a right to refuse to do a procedure that she morally or religiously objects to?

Also, who are doctors to judge? They are often human arbiters of life and death, simply by the merit of the prestige of their position and the power entrusted to them—they are the experts and they are in charge. But sometimes doctors are wrong. And not only the patient and the patient's family have to live with (or not live with) the consequences of a poor call made by the doctor, so too does the doctor.

There's also the question of recommending or performing life-sustaining therapy that the doctor knows will not, ultimately, extend life or improve life in any meaningful way. Is it ethical to give false hope to the patient and family? Is it moral to cause a patient or a patient's family to rack up medical bills and medical debt for something so futile? Or does a doctor have an obligation to be frank and honest with the patient? If the goal is patient autonomy and doing no harm, then probably the most objectively ethical action is to provide the opinion that the life-saving surgery will do no good. But if the patient still wishes to undergo that treatment, then that is the patient's decision. There's no guilt on the part of the doctor, and the patient's wishes have been met.

Codified Virtues

In 1974, the National Commission for the Protection of Human Subjects of Biomedical and Behavioral Research met to determine and solidify the primary virtues for medical and psychological research that involves humans. The three virtues initially agreed upon were autonomy, beneficence, and justice. Some members have personally adopted the additional virtues of non-maleficence, human dignity, and the sanctity of life.

Indeed, one of the prevailing opinions in medical ethics is a commitment to patient autonomy. This is a belief that patients have the right to do whatever they wish with their bodies. That includes eschewing medical care that the patient may be morally opposed to receiving. Indeed, some religions forbid life-saving blood transfusions, and doctors would have to respect a patient's decision to refuse that care.

CHALLENGES IN BIOETHICS

New Frontiers in Science and Philosophy

Bioethics is a combined word, joining "biology" with "ethics." It's a field that looks into the ethical and moral questions that have arisen, and continue to develop, in the field of biotechnology. Biotechnology is the ever-changing and ever-advancing field where cutting-edge science and/or gadgetry is applied to make the natural world function better or more efficiently. Examples of biotechnology, particularly ones that lead to bioethical analysis, include the development of genetically modified crops, how genetic information should be handled, and the rise of the idea of genetically enhanced "designer babies."

Making alterations to the natural world for a desired effect—as determined by an individual, a corporation, or a government—is naturally going to lead to some hand-wringing. Although the passage of time generally leads to greater acceptance of an idea, much in the field of biotechnology is so new that there's a good deal of ambiguity regarding what is "moral" or not.

Perhaps the loudest bioethical debate has to do with genetically modified organisms, or GMOs. Food scientists have been working for decades on using genetic engineering to create new varieties of tomatoes or corn, for example, that provide more flavor or that are more resistant to cold weather and insects, but only recently has the concern over genetic modifications come up. The main ethical problem is that the concept is, at its core, manipulating nature. Is it ethical to toy with the natural order of things? Regardless of whether it is or isn't, widespread GMO use could damage the environment, or lead to negative health benefits in humans. But GMOs are so relatively new that the long-term effects on earth or man are not yet fully known.

There's also the idea of owning nature. Is it morally okay for plants and organisms—albeit technologically enhanced ones—to be owned by a corporation? Could these modifications be viewed as evidence of human ingenuity, an example of making the world better and increasing happiness by making heartier food and more of it? But such ownership could also be seen as being disrespectful to the natural world, and such genetic modifications could be viewed as an exploitation of a living thing that has no say in the matter.

Views on Cloning

Although the first mammal was cloned more than twenty years ago—a sheep named Dolly, by scientists in Scotland—the technology to genetically replicate living things remains in its infancy. Changing public opinions about whether or not it is moral to do so have moved almost as slowly. According to a 2016 poll of Americans by the Pew Research Center, 81 percent think it's morally wrong to clone humans, and 60 percent said it's unethical to clone animals. When the poll was conducted in 2001, those numbers were at 88 and 63 percent, respectively.

Those in favor of GMOs cite some positives that could outweigh the potential negatives, even from an ethical standpoint. With the Earth's population rapidly increasing (7.5 billion and counting), the need for food rises just as quickly. GMO technology could be used to grow crops with high yields, little waste, or even with extra nutrition, making for a food supply that is much more efficient, stable, and plentiful. From an ethical standpoint, however, it's problematic and tricky to determine what's ethically "correct." Is it worth knowing what effect GMOs will have in the long run to our food supply and our planet, even as we allow their unfettered spread by for-profit companies so as to prevent millions from potentially starving?

SOCIAL ETHICS

How to Live in the Modern World

Moral philosophy is concerned with determining the virtues and reasons behind ethics. Laws are the practical, political, and codified applications of those ethics. Between those two systems are social ethics, the formal name for the moral standards, norms, and unofficial code of conduct that's expected from a person in the world, or in one's particular society, culture, or community.

Quotable Voices

"Education without values, as useful as it is, seems rather to make man a more clever devil." —C.S. Lewis

---

Social ethics are built on the shared values of many. But social values are different from those individual values. Individual values are virtues that each person seeks out for oneself, and they can be as varied as the person. These personal values don't necessarily become social values, nor do they become part of the framework that is social ethics. This is because of the intent of the value itself. Individual values, while virtuous and good (bravery, courage, and integrity are all examples) merely benefit the individual, or at least frame how that individual should lead his or her individual life. Social values, by contrast, are explicitly concerned with the welfare of others. The drive to help others—or even the abstract idea of "other people"—is what makes a value a social value. Having those social values in mind affects an individual's thoughts and behaviors. Individuals then take on these ethics, and that, in turn, helps build the social ethics of a society.

HOW SOCIAL ETHICS ARE CREATED

Obligations to others in a community is what drives social ethics. We have an obligation to help others, be they less fortunate or not, because sharing fuels society. Each of us is a part of society, and as we enjoy the benefits of living in that society, we are obligated to take part in it to help it function. Part of that is sharing, either directly via giving money or food to the less fortunate, for example, or indirectly, by using each of our unique talents and abilities to prop up one another, so that we may help society both operate and progress. Social accountability also factors into social ethics. Because we each have a role, we are trusted to fulfill that role, and thus we are accountable for our actions. This relationship between individual and society is precious and fragile, because other people are counting on you and your contributions to help make society hum. A refusal to play a part affects others—and it's unethical to impinge the happiness of others or to prevent them from living their best life.

While every society or culture has its ethical standards, how are these created or developed over time? Some factors include dominant religious beliefs, economic factors, and practicality. These prevailing social values are the ones that help a society meet its goals, particularly those that relate to peace and prosperity. Governmental organizations then respond to emerging norms by setting laws based on prevailing ethical standards. This can be a difficult task, however, as some of the more controversial topics in modern society are controversial specifically because their ethical nature is not clear-cut.

For the sake of comparison, take murder and assisted suicide. It's a universal moral norm that an individual taking the life of another human is wrong. But what about assisted suicide? There are several moral factors that complicate the issue. Some may find it extremely ethical to help another person achieve his or her goal—of ending a life beset with pain and sickness—out of the belief that humans should control their own destiny. Others may liken the practice to murder, because they believe that humans don't have the right to determine when life ends. Both are legitimate arguments within the field of ethics, but the laws about assisted suicide vary from place to place. In this instance, it is up to those in charge of the jurisdiction to consciously respond to the dominant moral opinions of the community and set the law that best reflects those concerns. This is how social ethics become laws and thus become ingrained as moral or ethical norms.

INDEX